THE COLLECTED WORKS OF JOHN BRANDANE:
THE ONE-ACT PLAYS

*John Brandane*

**The Treasure Ship and other Full-Length Plays**
The Glen is Mine (1923)
The Treasure Ship (1924)
The Lifting (1925)
The Inn of Adventure (1932)
Heather Gentry (1932)

**Rory Aforesaid and other One-Act Plays**
Glenforsa (1921) *with Alec Wilson Yuill*
The Change-House (1921)
Rory Aforesaid (1928)
The Happy War (1928)
The Spanish Galleon (1932) *with Alec Wilson Yuill*
Man of Uz (1932)

**Three Novels**
My Lady of Aros (1910)
The Captain More (1923)
Strawfeet (1930)

THE COLLECTED WORKS OF JOHN BRANDANE
VOLUME 2

# Rory Aforesaid
## and other
## One-Act Plays

*Glenforsa**
*The Change-House*
*Rory Aforesaid*
*The Happy War*
*The Spanish Galleon**
*Man of Uz*

## John Brandane
*with Alec Wilson Yuill

K&B
Kennedy & Boyd

Kennedy & Boyd
an imprint of
Zeticula Ltd
Unit 13,
196 Rose Street,
Edinburgh,
EH2 4AT

http://www.kennedyandboyd.co.uk
admin@kennedyandboyd.co.uk

First published:
Glenforsa (1921) with Alec Wilson Yuill
The Change-House (1921)
Rory Aforesaid (1928)
The Happy War (1928)
The Spanish Galleon (1932) with Alec Wilson Yuill
Man of Uz (1932)
This edition Copyright © Zeticula Ltd 2022
First published in this edition 2022

ISBN 978-1-84921-155-0

# Contents

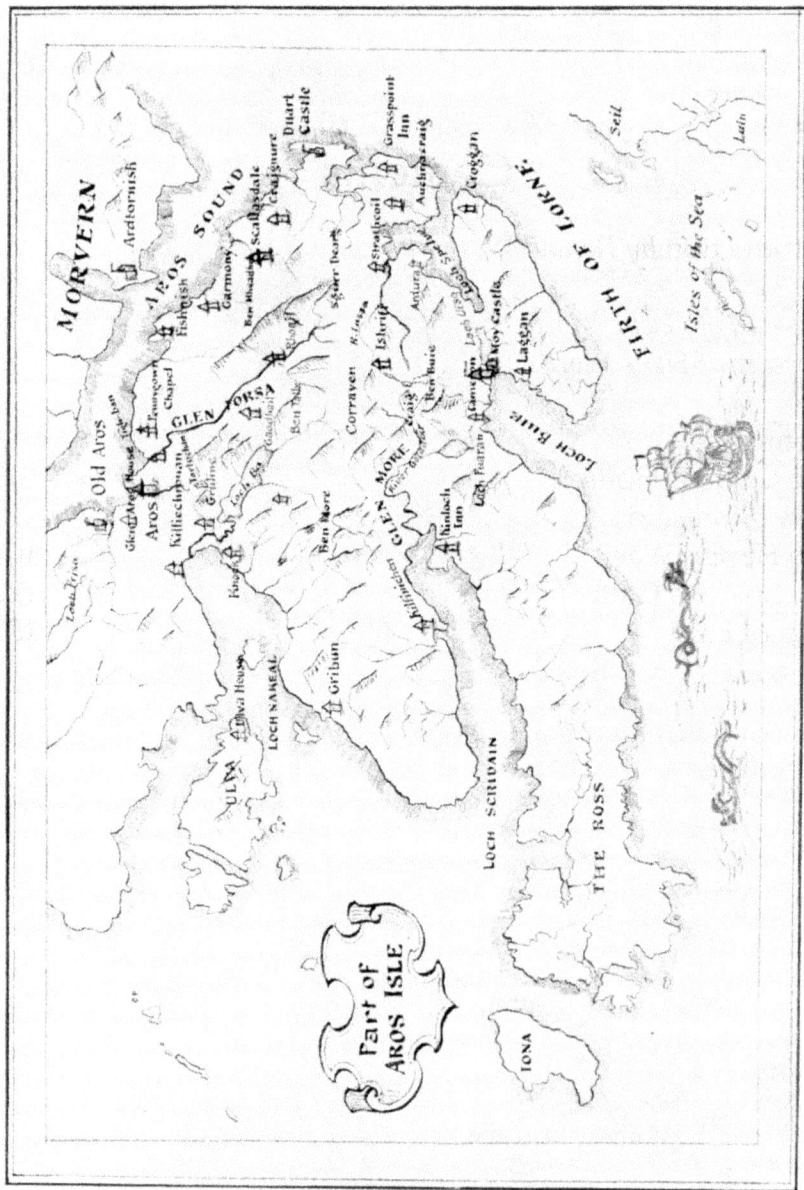

*Map used by Ian Fraser in his Journeyings in the Isle of Aros, A.D. 1759*

# Introduction

*John Brandane (1869-1947)*
*dramatist and novelist*

John Brandane (the pen name for Dr John MacIntyre) was arguably
Scotland's best known resident dramatist in the 1920s before the emergence
of that other great doctor/dramatist James Bridie (O. H. Mavor).

He was born in Rothesay on the Isle of Bute on 14ᵗʰ August, 1869. His
family moved to the Bridgeton area of Glasgow and as a boy he worked
in a Glasgow cotton mill. Between the ages of 15 and 27 he was employed
as a clerk in a warehouse. During his latter years in the warehouse he took
up the study of medicine at Glasgow University. In 1901 he graduated
and while specialising in surgery at Glasgow Royal Infirmary he met
and became a friend of Bridie. Since he had not taken a holiday for six
years, for the sake of his health he obtained his first medical post in a
rural practice on the Island of Mull and remained there until 1908.

His first known venture into literature is a long short story called "In Aros
Isle" which he wrote in 1905. With advice on its plot and characterisation
and praise for its "zest" from Neil Munro this developed into the novel
*My Lady of Aros* which was published in 1910. Its setting is the location for
almost all of Brandane's later work —Eilean Aros, or Aros Isle — a thinly
disguised Island of Mull. Like Neil Munro's *Shoes of Fortune*, it deals with
the abortive Jacobite Rising of 1759 and treachery -in this case the treachery
of the heroine's double dealing spy brother Norman.

From 1908 until 1912 Brandane moved to England and was a general
practitioner in a rural area in the Thames Valley. While there he paid
occasional visits to London where performances by the Abbey Theatre
Players from Dublin turned his mind towards writing drama. In 1912 he
returned to Glasgow and remained in general practice in the Hyndland
area until 1935. During WW1 he served as surgeon in a hospital in the
French sector of the Western Front at Arc-en-Barrois near Verdun.

When he returned to live in Glasgow he was to become deeply
involved in the city's theatrical life. He renewed his acquaintance with
A W Yuill and together they pushed the cause for a native Scottish

drama and began writing for the Scottish National Players. His first one act play (with Yuill), *Glenforsa* (1921), portrays a spirited and drunken quarrel between two friends, Glenforsa and Oskamull, the gambling away of Glenforsa's Mull properties and the romantic entanglement of the two men with two sisters. This was followed by another one act play *The Change House.* In 1922, when he was 53 years old, he became a founder member of the Scottish National Players and in effect their in-house dramatist since almost all of his plays were performed by them.

1923 saw the performance of what is probably his most important full length play *The Glen is Mine.* This work has good characterisation and a strong theme, the future of the Highlands: are industry and progress preferable to the destruction of the old Highland way of life? The ending, however, shies away from a bold resolution and opts for a safer, more sentimental conclusion. In 1923 he also published the novel *The Captain More,* a re-working and extension of the ideas of his play *Glenforsa.*

1924 saw the performance of the full length romantic comedy *The Treasure Ship* with its background of the salvaging of treasure from a Spanish galleon supposedly sunk in Tobermory Bay. In 1925 *The Lifting* (a development of the one act *The Change House*) a full length play full of irony and coincidence set in the south of Mull near Lochbuie goes back to the period of 1745 Jacobite Rising. It demonstrates the honour and decency of the hero Iain in sacrificing his life to protect the friend whom he had inadvertently implicated in the killing of an "enemy" before the beginning of the play.

In 1926 Tyrone Guthrie directed Brandane's one act comedy masterpiece *Rory Aforesaid* with its wily elderly protagonist. This was followed by the grim and ironic one act *The Happy War* (1928) set in war-torn France, the full length comedy *Heather Gentry* (1932), the historical one act *The Spanish Galleon* (1932) (again co-authored with Yuill) which deals with the sinking of the galleon in Tobermory Bay and *The Inn of Adventure* (1932), a stage adaptation of the novel *The Captain More.* His final play, *The Man of Uz* (1938), is a verse drama of the suffering of Job.

Perhaps, outside his plays, the most interesting achievement of his later literary work is his third and final novel *Strawfeet* (1930). This deals with the First World War and is set partly on Mull and partly in France on the Western Front. Like *My Lady of Aros* it deals again with espionage and betrayal but this time in contemporary life. Brandane is one of the few Scots to have written a novel dealing with the First World War. And he dedicated it to Neil Munro, "Master of those who know the Gael".

In 1935 he found the demands of medical practice in the city and authorship too heavy. He returned to the Highlands to rural practice in Lochgoilhead in Argyll. He died there on 17<sup>th</sup> October, 1947.

# Glossary of Gaelic Words

| | |
|---|---|
| *Aghmhor* | happy |
| *Albainn* | Scotland |
| *Amadan* | fool |
| *An Gillie Dubh* | The Dark-haired lad |
| *Beannachd leat (singular)* | Blessing on you, goodbye |
| *Beannachd leibh (plural))* | |
| *Beag* | little |
| *Bodach* | old man |
| *Caileag bheag* | little girl |
| *Cailleach* | old woman |
| *Cailleachean* | old women |
| *Canach* | wild cotton |
| *Canntaireachd* | chaunt |
| *Cas-chrom* | plough |
| *Cibeir* | shepherd |
| *Ceilidh* | story-telling, gossip, folk tales |
| *Clachan* | a group of cottages |
| *Cladh Phobuill* | The Burying Place of the People (or Tribe) |
| *Clarsach* | Highland harp |
| *Cnoc-na-croiche* | Gallows-Hill |
| *Co tha sin?* | Who is there? |
| *Cogadh no Sith* | War or Peace |
| *Creach* | spoil, plunder |
| *Crodh Chailein* | Colin's cattle |
| *Crotnag* | shepherd's crook |
| *Cuach* | cup, wooden bowl |
| *Cuarain* | foot-covering of the raw hide |
| *Dhia!* | God! |
| *Direach sin!* | Just so! |
| *Drammach* | meal and water |
| *Dugh* | dark |

| | |
|---|---|
| *Duin'-uasal* | gentleman |
| *Eilean* | isle |
| *Eilean Dhia* | isle of God |
| *Feasgar math!* | Good evening! |
| *Fin McCoul* | Legendary Gaelic hero |
| *Fleurisch* | Flint and steel |
| *Garron* | Highland pony |
| *Ghaol mo chridhe!* | White love of my heart |
| *Gillie* | a lad, a Highland commoner |
| *ille!* | lad |
| *Iorraman* | boat-songs |
| *Laochain* | my hero |
| *Maam* | a round, steep hill |
| *Mainnir nam Fiadh* | The Playground of the Deer (a hill) |
| *Marbh phaisg ort!* | Death-wrapping be on thee! |
| *M'eudail!* | My treasure! |
| *Mallachd ort!* | Curse on you! |
| *Mo chridhe!* | My dear! |
| *Mo thruaigh!* | My sorrow! |
| *Mogain* | footless stockings |
| *Och, ille, ille* | Oh, lad, lad! |
| *Och, ochan!* | Alas, alas! |
| *Och, ubh, ubh!* | Oh, dear, dear! |
| *Oidche mhath!* | Good night! |
| *Ruapais* | The Careless One, the Rigmarole |
| *Sassenach* | Southerner |
| *Seanachaidhean* | story-tellers, bards |
| *seilisders* | sedges |
| *Sgalag* | ploughman |
| *Sgian dubh* | black knife |
| *Slainte mhath!* | Good health! |
| *Slainte mhor mhath!* | Great health! |
| *Slan lea!* | Farewell! |
| *Suas e ... suas e* | up with it ... up with it |
| *Taghairm* | invocation (of spirits) |
| *Tearlach* | Charles |
| *Tearlach Og* | Prince Charlie |
| *Thoir an aire!* | Look out! |
| *Tir-nan-Oig* | Land of the Ever-Young |
| *Tonnag* | a small shawl |

# Glossary of Scots Words

| | |
|---|---|
| *Airt* | direction |
| *Bannock* | scone |
| *Bawbee* | halfpenny |
| *Body* | person |
| *Bouman* | cowman, or crofter |
| *Breaking* | bankruptcy |
| *Brock* | beast |
| *Causey* | causeway |
| *Cogie* | wooden bowl |
| *Craig* | throat |
| *Cruisie* | metal lamp |
| *Deave* | deafen |
| *Doer* | agent |
| *Ettled* | intended |
| *Fleeching.* | scolding |
| *Girning* | complaining peevishly |
| *Gowff* | gust |
| *Greetin'* | bewailing |
| *Hamesucken* | assaulting a person with violence in his own house. |
| *Haud* | hold |
| *Haud till't!* | Hold on! |
| *Howe and corrie* | hollow and height |
| *instrument o' sasine* | An attestation by a Notary Public certifying the bargain. |
| *Jalouse* | surmise |
| *Jo* | lover |
| *Lave* | remainder |
| *Loon* | fellow |
| *Maun* | must |
| *Mirk* | dark |
| *Oxter* | armpit |

| | |
|---|---|
| *Scunner* | disgust |
| *Scrape, the* | the 'Forty-five Rising |
| *Shaw* | thicket, plantations |
| *Skirling* | shrieking |
| *Smeddum* | spirit |
| *Snood* | a ribbon for the hair |
| *Soumings* | allotments |
| *Spate* | flood |
| *Spier* | enquire |
| *Spring* | lively tune |
| *Stravaging* | wandering |
| *Tacks of land* | portions of land |
| *Tacksman* | a lessee of land who sublets to crofters |
| *Thrapple* | windpipe |
| *Tinchel* | hunt |
| *Tocher* | marriage portion |
| *Trusty* | secret agent |
| *Tyke* | dog |
| *Wadset* | a pawning of land |
| *Warlock* | wizard |

# Glenforsa

## Persons of the Play

MacKinnon of Glenforsa ⟩ *Young Highland Lairds*
MacDougall of Oskamull⟩

Elspeth Cameron    *Daughter of Cameron of Draolinn.*

Anna MacDougall    *Kinswoman and Housekeeper to Oskamull.*

Time  1760
Place  Eilean Aros (Inner Hebrides).
Scene  The Salle at Oskamull.


*First produced by the Scottish National Players for the St. Andrew Society at the Royal Institute, Glasgow, on Thursday, 13th January 1921, with the following cast:*

| | |
|---|---|
| Glenforsa | Major R. B. Wharrie. |
| Elspeth | Miss Cathie Fletcher. |
| Oskamull | Captain J. Ronald Young. |
| Anna | Miss Elliot C. Mason. |

*The play produced by* Mr. Andrew P. Wilson.

SCENE: *The Salle of Oskamull House in the West Highlands, late on an October night in the year 1760. A large chamber, sombre, time-worn, serving as library and dining-room. It contains some old book-cases, stagheads, and devices of arms on the walls; deer and seal skins on the floor of dark wood. Behind are two windows, heavily curtained, with an estate chart hanging between them. The night-wind moans outside. A door L leads into the Hall, and another door R into a back passage. To the right is a large fireplace with a peat fire burning; and on the other side a heavy sideboard with decanter, glasses, and writing-material. Small tables, chairs, and couch of strong, rude type. Playing cards and dice on one of the tables. Candlesticks with lighted candles on sideboard and mantle-piece.*

KENNETH MACDOUGALL, *the Laird of Oskamull, in a kilt suit of crotal, without plaid, but wearing a sword, is moving about restlessly. He is a fresh-complexioned, open, frank, impulsive young fellow, with lean, well-formed features, fair hair and freckled brow. The aged housekeeper, also present, had nursed him as a child, and it is somewhat vainly that he tries to impress her with his authority.*

ANNA MACDOUGALL, *the housekeeper, a poor relation of the Laird, is tending the fire and candles. She is about seventy; pale, wrinkled, and thick-set; but moves about with a light foot. Her dress is of dark material and she wears a tartan screen on her shoulders, fastened with a large Celtic brooch. She chatters at her tasks, and is annoyed that the Laird gives so little heed to her.*

#### ANNA

But it's not one word or two would silence the like of Morag. It's just Glenforsa's the great gallant, says she. A lie has only one leg to stand on, and, if the story wasn't true, it wouldn't have travelled so far.

#### OSKAMULL

*(Impatiently.)* I wish you'd mind the old word of our folks to keep a knot on the tongue. It's Glenforsa I'm expecting even now.

#### ANNA

*(Surprised.)* Glenforsa.

#### OSKAMULL

Yes, yes. *(Impatiently and trying to assert his authority.)* And it's a matter of some moment, look you, or I wouldn't be asking you to bide up so late.

#### ANNA

*(Concerned.)* Oh, I hope it will not be the cartes again, Oskamull. *Och, ochan!* it will be no affair of mine ... but the way the young lairds are gambling their money and their lands! What I'm seeing is this, the old lands and the green glens, and the kindly folk on them, pawned to the greedy Sassenach.

**OSKAMULL**

*(Haughtily.)* There's no talk of cartes. Glenforsa is coming with a lady.

**ANNA**

*(Amazed and dropping the candle-snuffers.)* A lady with Glenforsa, at this hour of dark! ... after the way he's been toying with Draolinn's two daughters?

**OSKAMULL**

Well ... to please you ... it's one of them he's coming with ... Grizel.

**ANNA**

*(Astounded.)* Grizel!

**OSKAMULL**

*(On his dignity.)* What for will you be staring at me? It's no concern of mine.

**ANNA**

Shame on you, Oskamull! to be encouraging him in the like of this. It's to be quit of him you do it.

**OSKAMULL**

*(Flushing and trying to hide it under a show of indignation.)* How should I want to be quit of him.

**ANNA**

It's no secret to whisper behind the door what you think of her sister Elspeth ... who's eating her heart out for Glenforsa, though it's cruelly he deserted her. And she's too old for a young lad like you.

**OSKAMULL**

Your tongue's like a loose thatch-rope on a windy day. Glenforsa's my friend, look you, and maybe has reasons for his wildness. Though he has no love to our clan, there's not a truer heart in all the Isles. It's not for us to decide his love-affairs. He's old enough to look after himself.

**ANNA**

It's helping him you are, in order to set Elspeth free for yourself.

**OSKAMULL**

*(Impatiently.)* Tcha! I'm going down to step the mast in the boat, for it's crossing the Loch he'll be. You can tell him to make the place his own till I come back.

*(He goes out R.*

**ANNA**

*(Putting peats on the fire.)* Oh, the young lairds, the young lairds ... It's plucking the bitter sloe they are, and trampling the honeycomb. Whatna road is it, at all, at all, our feet are on?

*(Hearing a sound she crosses to the door L, and, opening it, admits Glenforsa and a Lady, whose face is hidden under a veil and the hood of her cloak. The cavalier is in tight-fitting trews of a dark hunting tartan, and his long plaid is of the same tartan. He has dark, firm-set, handsome features, on which sits a strained and anxious expression. His bearing is proud and a little abrupt. He wears a sword.*

**GLENFORSA**

Good evening, Anna.

**ANNA**

*(Not too graciously.)* Good evening, sir.

**GLENFORSA**

Has the Chief returned?

**ANNA**

Yes. He's gone down to the Lochside ... and you were to make the house your own till he came back.

**GLENFORSA**

Thanks. Here's the cheering blaze. Go over and warm yourself, Grizel, while I see to the horses. Tearlach has injured himself— knocked his leg against a tree in the dark.

*(He goes out L.*

**ANNA**

Won't you come up to the fire, Grizel? Kenneth has just been telling me about you.

*(The Lady unveils and throws back her hood.*
*(Astounded.)* Mo thruaigh! Elspeth, is it you?

**ELSPETH**

*(Glancing round in alarm.)* Hush! Don't let him hear you.

**ANNA**

Ochan, ochanee! Will you tell me that he doesn't know?

**ELSPETH**

*(With clenched hand at her lips.)* He doesn't. He could see nothing in the darkness.

**ANNA**

My grief and my sorrow, lass! Whatna gate is this you go?

**ELSPETH**

*(Distractedly.)* He had planned to meet ... and run off with Grizel. It was pitch-black in the wood and I took her place. It was the only way to stop her. We have not exchanged words in all that wild ride ... How I'm trembling!

**ANNA**

My poor dear, let me bring you a warm bite and sup.

**ELSPETH**

Nothing, Anna ... Nothing.

**ANNA**

This is a sorry thing you're doing. What provoked you to it?

**ELSPETH**

Mad, I think ... But I tell you there was no other way to shield her from him. It's done ... whatever.

**ANNA**

I know the regard you have for him; though, Guid kens, with little reason.

**ELSPETH**

It wasn't for that ... He's spoiled my life. Could I sit idle and see the same happen to Grizel? ... Though what's to come of me now? *(Pauses perplexed.)*

**ANNA**

I thought your father wouldna let Glenforsa come near the house.

**ELSPETH**

He has not been ... Grizel met him at my Uncle Donald's in the Black Isle. You know how wilful she is.

**ANNA**

You did right to stop her. She's too young to be going her own roads yet. But it's fell sorry I am for you, Elspeth ... wearing your soul out for the like of him.

**ELSPETH**

That wasn't in my mind, I tell you.

**ANNA**

Maybe no; but it's hard to forget. Don't I see it in your wasted eyes and the trouble that is on you?

**ELSPETH**

*(Pained.)* Well, well. Isn't it the way with us women, for weal or woe?

**ANNA**

If I could only help you, lass.

**ELSPETH**

*(Starting.)* I hear his foot.

**ANNA**

*(Trying to comfort her.)* Come to my room, *mo chridhe*. I'll tell him. His anger will fall light on me.

**ELSPETH**

*(With quiet resolution.)* I've brought this on myself and I'll see it through.
*(She again veils herself.*

**ANNA**

But the black rage that will be on him!

**ELSPETH**

I'm not afraid of him. And what does it matter for me now?
*(Glenforsa re-enters L.*

**GLENFORSA**

Two of the horses are foundered. The roads are vile.

**ANNA**

*(Screening Elspeth.)* If you'll take something to eat, sir—though the lady will not—there's wine and venison on the board.

**GLENFORSA**

Nothing! *(Impatiently.)* ... Nothing. Leave us, Anna.

**ANNA**

*(Loath to withdraw.)* And there's meat of each meat and drink of each drink for the asking.

**GLENFORSA**

*(Waving her off)* No, nothing ... but I thank you. *(Takes off plaid)*
*( Anna goes out R.*
Come into the light and warmth, Grizel. Why are you lingering there? The nip of that wind's in my bones. You're not timid, are you, after the pluck you've shown? Faith! I was in mortal fear for you at the cliffs of Kellan. The salt spray blinded me, and I heard the sea thundering at our feet.
*(Elspeth steps quickly forward and touches a peat on the fire.*
*(With a laugh)* What old freit's this ... touching fire? Surely it's not from me you would seek sanctuary? There's none of your clan about. Take off your cloak, my lass, and let me see you smiling bravely.
*(Elspeth unveils in the light.*
God shield us! Elspeth? *(Starting back.)*

**ELSPETH**

Yes.

**GLENFORSA**

What devil's trick is this? *(After a pause.)* Speak, woman, if woman ye be. Why have ye done this?

**ELSPETH**

(*Quietly.*) I did it ... to save my sister.

**GLENFORSA**

To save her?

**ELSPETH**

Yes, from you. And maybe you'll guess what made me so desperate.

**GLENFORSA**

No, faith, it's beyond me ... unless from the petty spite of a jealous woman.

**ELSPETH**

(*With a bitter laugh.*) Jealous?

**GLENFORSA**

Yes. They say a woman can still be jealous after being false to a man.

**ELSPETH**

You dare say that to me? I love my sister Grizel ... and what would I be doing but try to protect her from a broken man taking advantage of her youth?

**GLENFORSA**

(*Bitterly.*) Aye, broken, you say, without giving a thought to the cause of it. By what witch's craft did you get your sister to consent to this?

**ELSPETH**

She had no hand in it. Old Flora told me your plans. I went to the trysting-place, and Grizel was directed ... elsewhere.

**GLENFORSA**

Where was she sent to?

**ELSPETH**

To Sron-na-Cranalich.

**GLENFORSA**

You left her in that lonely wood and dark, to the cry of the raven and the night hag ... and the deer so wild on the hill? The cruelty of it! In her grief and disappointment.

**ELSPETH**

It's not Grizel would be scared by a deer-horn, and she's too young to feel so very deeply ... And how could you have any regard for a *caileag bheag*, the like of her?

**GLENFORSA**

After worshipping a woman so queenly as yourself?

**ELSPETH**

There was little pretence in the regard you once had for me.

**GLENFORSA**

My pain and my longing! I've known the day when my thoughts of you rankled—misery enough and to spare! But Grizel helped me to forget ... though it's like you she is in a hundred little tricks of the lip and eye.

**ELSPETH**

*(With a tremulous laugh, for she sees what this implies.)* Yes, yes. It's me that kens.

**GLENFORSA**

Oh, you may laugh! but I had the best of reasons for putting you out of my mind.

**ELSPETH**

And me no less.

**GLENFORSA**

*(In an angry outburst.)* You were blithe enough to take up with young Oskamull as soon as my back was turned on the Isles.

**ELSPETH**

That's untrue.

**GLENFORSA**

You would deny it? Never a word came from you in answer to my letters ... while you were to be seen with him everywhere at market, kirk and hunt-meet.

**ELSPETH**

You were always the knowing one, Alan ... a quick eye for the faults of others, a blind one for your own ... How long was I left without word or message from you in the sorest trial of my life? Oskamull was the good friend to us when the trouble began in the Isles. It was in black despair at you deserting me that I gave in to my father's wish.

**GLENFORSA**

Aye, it was easy casting off a despised and broken gamester.

**ELSPETH**

I never called you gamester, but the whole world kens you were roystering and gaming when other men had to stake their lives.

**GLENFORSA**

That's what my enemies say of me. I expected something else from you. I knew the folly of attempting another Rising and did my best to stop it. Duel after duel was forced on me, for so they tried to cut me off ... and there was I, sword to sword against the men my whole wish was to save.

**ELSPETH**

(*Amazed and gazing at him.*) Alan! I never heard of this!

**GLENFORSA**

No, your father would take good care of that. At Dalkeith I got a rapier-thrust, and lay for a long time at death's door. Your Aunt in Edinburgh was the good friend to me and promised to send you word. I know she's not the one to play me false.

**ELSPETH**

(*Staggered by this.*) Aunt Janet?

**GLENFORSA**

Yes, she promised to get my letters through to you from the Low Countries.

**ELSPETH**

Oh! (*Going aside in anguish.*)

**GLENFORSA**

What's come to you? Didn't she do it?

**ELSPETH**

She went out of her mind when her son, young Ronald, was shot as a rebel.

**GLENFORSA**

Out of her mind? And you received no message?

**ELSPETH**

Neither word nor script.

**GLENFORSA**

(*Wistfully.*) Elspeth!

**ELSPETH**

Grizel told you nothing?

**GLENFORSA**

It's often she would be speaking of you, but I turned a deaf ear to any mention of your name. When I came back you might have made some advance.

**ELSPETH**

It was too much for my pride. (*With a laugh.*) And for yours too, I'm thinking,

**GLENFORSA**

H'm! ... Then, Elspeth, *mo chridhe*, now we understand —

**ELSPETH**

My mind's in a coil. ... I don't know what to do.

**GLENFORSA**

Trust yourself to me, white love of my heart! ... Let us go at once before your father comes near.

**ELSPETH**

*(Distractedly.)* My father! ... Oh, it's not him I should be leaving in this way ... him that's getting up in years! ... And Grizel! ... Oh, it's for her my heart is wae.

**GLENFORSA**

You know what it will be if your father and I meet?

**ELSPETH**

Too well! ... But I must have time to think ... I should do something to soften him ... something to comfort my sister.

*(Voices heard in the hall.*

*(Starting.)* Who's that?

**GLENFORSA**

It's Oskamull ... He was expecting us.

**ELSPETH**

Oh! Why did I come here? ... I've been so rash! ... I mustn't ... I can't see him now!

**GLENFORSA**

What does it matter? ... You don't trust me then?

**ELSPETH**

It's not that, Alan ... But I've been reckless ... unthinking ... It's to my ain folk my mind's turning ... Oh! It's no easy thing to take the whole world for your pillow.

**GLENFORSA**

*(Haughtily.)* Then, it's more afraid you are of offending Oskamull than wrecking every hope of mine?

**ELSPETH**

No, no, Alan ... but ... give me time ... I must have some feeling for my kith and kin ... Maybe Anna could help me ... I'll go to Anna.

*(Glenforsa turns away, stung with disappointment. Elspeth looks round—*
*hesitates—and goes quickly off R. Glenforsa looks after her, then tosses his*
*head and laughs bitterly. He walks to the sideboard and lifts a decanter of wine.*
*Oskamull comes in L.*

**OSKAMULL**

You're here, Alan. *(With a laugh.)* Sound, I hope, in wind and limb. It's the wild ploy you're on; and a savage night and a cold for it. The moon is swimming through clouds like a platter in the waves. There'll be the devil to pay in giving you aid and comfort, *ille*; for old Draolinn's the thrawn one! ... and yet, and yet, it might have been myself that was at the same market ... for, in your lug, it's the great liking I have for some of the Draolinn folk ... *(Laughs.)* Indeed, Alan, I thought it was Elspeth you had your eye on, and it's been a great relief to me to find it's Grizel. Where is she? Resting?

**GLENFORSA**

*(Evading an answer as he drinks.)* Good Burgundy, *ille*! ... You'll forgive me making free with it. I've fed on nothing but the night-wind. *Slainte mhòr mhath!*

**OSKAMULL**

It's an adventure to tear at the nerves, and I'll not be wondering you're upset.
                    *(Glenforsa pours out another glass and gulps it down.*
But easy, *laochain!* Remember who has confided herself to your keeping ... And, if you've to cross the loch before the mouth of day, you'll need your weather eye unshuttered ... Just listen to that blast—one of Fin McCoul's wildest.

**GLENFORSA**

There's not much crossing will be done by me this night, I'm thinking.

**OSKAMULL**

You're welcome to my roof, lad, and all below it ... And yet it's safer you'd be with the broad waters of Loch-na-Keal between you and old Draolinn with his gillies.

**GLENFORSA**

*(Drinking again.)* Slainte mhath,*ille!* and may your fortunes be as straight as mine have been crooked.

**OSKAMULL**

*(Watching him narrowly.)* What's come to you, Glenforsa? Is anything wrong?

**GLENFORSA**

Well, *laochain*, it's always a puzzle to a man to discover that a woman, after all, is only a woman ... And I'll not be hiding from you that there have been some words between the lady and myself ... So let's talk of something else.

**OSKAMULL**

It's fell sorry I will be to hear it, Alan ... But you must make some allowance, man ... It's a great wrench for a girl the like of Grizel, and she's bound to have after-thoughts ... You mustn't be minding any hasty words of hers at such a time ... And I'll wager you—yes, I'll wager it will only be a matter of minutes before she's back, pleading with you to forgive and forget.

**GLENFORSA**

Kenneth, lad, you have the wisdom of Conan himself. *Slainte mhath! (Holding up his glass again.)* Here's to your great knowledge of womankind! *(Then in a sudden passion.)* But let me be getting my thoughts off it, or the blood will be bursting from my veins! *(He moves restlessly about.)*

**OSKAMULL**

Content ye, man! Indeed, indeed, it is a nerve-wracking affair. But sit ye down and make yourself at ease. Won't ye take something to eat?

**GLENFORSA**

*(Waving it off with a gesture.)* You were talking of wagering a moment since ... You've the cartes here. *(Going to table.)* Or better still, there's dice. *(Lifting the dice he spills a pack of cards on the floor.)* Let's try a main. I must have something to keep me from thinking, or I'll be going crazed!

**OSKAMULL**

No dicing to-night, Alan! I've had too much of that these days ... Besides—this is barely the time for it.

**GLENFORSA**

*(With some bitterness.)* You were ready enough at Duart; but then you had all the luck!

**OSKAMULL**

At Duart! It was just there I had no wish to be winning. Indeed, at the last, I was staking high to lose, but it only added to my gains.

**GLENFORSA**

*(Sarcastically.)* Just so!

**OSKAMULL**

Oh? If you think I owe you your revenge! ... But it must be only a round or two.

*(They sit down at a table.)*

Your throw first.

#### GLENFORSA

Seven's the main! ... Let's stake ten yellow Geordies ... *(With a bitter laugh.)* It's as good a use as I'll find for them, since wedding-jaunts are out of fashion!

*(They play.*
Trey! ... They're yours, lad. You're drinking nothing. It's your cast.

#### OSKAMULL

It's nothing I'll be wanting at present ... I'll call five.

#### GLENFORSA

Chance to you ... Chance again ... They're yours... Other ten? ... Seven's the main for me once more.

#### OSKAMULL

Eleven nicks to seven ... They're yours.

#### GLENFORSA

Mine? Good ... I'll set you fifty this time. You take them?

#### OSKAMULL

Yes ... Nine's the main.

#### GLENFORSA

Cinque, quatre! ... Gone too! ... Ha-ha!

#### OSKAMULL

The stakes are too high.

#### GLENFORSA

Not they ... I'll double you for the next throw ... a hundred Geordies — unless — your nerves?

#### OSKAMULL

Go on.

#### GLENFORSA

Five's the main! ... There! ... Yours also.

#### OSKAMULL

There's no need for such big stakes, Glenforsa ... Let's be moderate.

#### GLENFORSA

No, by the Rood! ... They'll be higher yet, *ille* ... I'm in the mood to make a spoon or spoil a horn... There ... that's the bottom of my pouch ... But I'll tell you what—
*(He rises, and, going to the chart on the wall, sets his finger on it.*
I'll stake Ben Talla and all the clachans between it and Forsa against Cairn More with its bog and bracken—if you've pluck enough.

**OSKAMULL**

Is it mad you are?

**GLENFORSA**

Is it timid you are—with an unslaked gullet?

**OSKAMULL**

I'll make some negus *(Rising, he goes to the door and calls.)* Anna! ... Anna!

**GLENFORSA**

Ben Talla against Cairn More, my buck!

*(Anna comes in L.*

**OSKAMULL**

Bring hot water, Anna, and some sugar.

*( Anna goes out R.*

A fig for timidity. I'll take you. Six is the main.

**GLENFORSA**

Right, my bantling! It's your throw ... Good tacks against scrub oak
and moorland ... Twelve nicks to six. Yours ... ha! Well, you've the
devil's own luck this night!

*(He goes to the map and makes a mark with a quill.*

**OSKAMULL**

Better stop.

**GLENFORSA**

There will be no stopping now.

*(Enter Anna with tray, etc. R.*

Ben Talla—the stags in every corrie, and the eagle's nest I harried when
a boy—the crofts at Gaodhail ... all gone for a throw of the dice coggie
... Ha-ha! ... Well, there's still the Hill of the Two Winds, and Mainnir
nam Fiadh.

**ANNA**

Oskamull! It's at the dicing you are after all! ... Gentlemen, gentlemen!
Stop you for the Good Being's sake! *Och, ubh! ubh!* It's sacrilege and
profanation to gamble away the 'very hills of God!' ... the bread and life
of the good kindly people!

**OSKAMULL**

*(With the gamester's preoccupation.)* Set down the stoups, Anna, and leave us.

**GLENFORSA**

*(Gruffly.)* Go away, old woman! *Mallachd ort!* ... But still and on it's the
true word you have ... Yet what for should I be listening to you? Your
sex can cozen out the souls of men—and what's a wheen rocks and
sticks to that, will you tell me? Oskamull, *ille,* your estate's but a small

15

one: there are lowland farms I ken would make two of it. But here's the magic stone will make a real chieftain of you. *(Flinging up the dice and catching it again in his palm.)* Here's the little mole will toss up mountain heights for you, whose tops darken the stars! Come ... Mainnir nam Fiadh—with the burial-place of my clan on it—against Ben Talla that's now yours. Damn! Gone too! The dead clansmen will avenge me! *(With a bitter laugh.)* You'll have them shambling up to your window at midnight and peering in on you with their eyeless skulls.

*(He rises and brings over his glass with Burgundy.* Well, well! They're saying that a farmer on his feet is taller than a chieftain on his knees.

### OSKAMULL
*(Making himself a drink.)* Will you have some negus?

### GLENFORSA
The Burgundy will do. *(Resuming his seat.)*

### ANNA
*Och, mo thruaigh, mo thruaigh!* That ever I should live to see the like! What's to become of the land if this is the gate you go? The grey witch of Maam is out on the wind this night, or Ewen with the Little Head ... for an evil spell's been put on you.

### OSKAMULL
Leave us, Anna, I tell you. If the hills go, I've still the little isles, woman.

### ANNA
*Mo thruaigh!* The Highlands, the old, old Highlands, what's to come of them and their folk, with their chiefs so heartless and so spendthrift. *Och, ubh, ubh!* ... This night! This night!

### OSKAMULL
Leave us, Anna, or must I be putting you out.

*(Anna goes out R.* Still, it's the true word she says, and it's best we should be stopping.

### GLENFORSA
No, by the cloven head of Ben Cruachan, I must conjure the Mainnir back, or as much of its soil as will cover my bones. So here's for the Hill of the Two Winds against it, *laochain!* Seven's the main, again!

*(They play.* Gone also! *(Throwing himself back in his chair and stretching up his arms.)* Now, look you, here's a pretty pickle for a Highlandman!

### OSKAMULL
Well, if you will persist in your folly ...

**GLENFORSA**

It's fighting we should be for the old lands, *ille* ... and would, my dear, if the great good days were back, when a man could make or unmake himself with a sword-stroke.

**OSKAMULL**

(*Bridling.*) You forced the play on me, Glenforsa, and well you know it was none of my choosing.

**GLENFORSA**

Oh, I'm not grudging you your gains, my hero ... Why, man, I'm in a mood to toss for the stars of Heaven! And truth to tell, there's a lady under your roof-tree whose beauty would dim their light. Here, Kenneth ... let's try a main for her—as gangrels toss for their trulls!

**OSKAMULL**

(*Beside himself with anger*) You go too far, sir! ... Are you out of your mind? Do you know what you're saying? An insult to Grizel Cameron is an insult to me!

**GLENFORSA**

(*Giving way to the full rancour of his jealousy.*) Damn you for a fool, Kenneth! What would I want with a gilp of a lass like Grizel? It's Elspeth herself that's here ... Elspeth on whom you've had the arrogance to throw a covetous eye!

**OSKAMULL**

(*Sitting back amazed.*) Elspeth! ... You hound! ... You dare to talk in such a fashion of her!

**GLENFORSA**

(*With ominous self-possession.*) And why will I not, comrade mine? Who but she has brought me to this pass, think you? And after her flight with me, is there anyone will look at her? It's in my power she has put herself, and why should I not use it, my pretty man?

**OSKAMULL**

Indeed, she's not in your power, my gentleman, and never will be!
(*He throws the contents of his glass in Glenforsa's face. Both men spring to their feet, drawing their swords, and upsetting chairs and table. Attracted by the noise, Anna comes in R and rushes out R calling for Elspeth. After a few passes Glenforsa disarms Oskamull who stands rigid confronting him.*)

**GLENFORSA**

(*Haughtily.*) Take up your sword, man. It's not your blood I'd be having, anyway.

**OSKAMULL**

*(Picking up his sword.)* I'm grateful, sir, for a second chance; for it's not at this we can stop. You've put an insult on me and on the lady who might have claimed your protection ... And that, ... well, that can only be wiped out in blood.

*(Elspeth comes in R and stands behind.)*

**GLENFORSA**

Tach! I'll not fight with you, laddie ... If chance is to settle what's between us, it will be better doing it with the dice.

**OSKAMULL**

*Thoir an aire!* Defend yourself!

**ELSPETH**

*(Interposing.)* Kenneth! ... For my sake, put up your sword.

**OSKAMULL**

It's grossly he has insulted you, and I beg you will withdraw.

**ELSPETH**

*(To Glenforsa.)* You would force a fight on him— a mere boy?

**GLENFORSA**

Boy? ... Aye, I daresay you're right in that ... But I'm shamed and outfaced by him, boy or no'. Well, I owe him reparation.

*(Making to handle his sword again.)*

**ELSPETH**

What sort of reparation will it be, if either of you is slain? Fools and blind!

**GLENFORSA**

Slain? *(With a laugh.)* Here's one has little care! Well, well! So let it be ... Well, Kenneth! I was in the wrong and I ask your pardon. *(Going to sideboard.)* Here are pens and paper handy. I'll give you a bond for your winnings ... It's your best revenge. When you think of it, death's a poor shabby bargain to strike in any cause.

**ELSPETH**

You've been at the dicing?

**GLENFORSA**

And he's the lucky one ... But it's little odds. I'll be shaking the dust of the Isles from my feet before the day's long awake.

**ELSPETH**

Leave us for a little, Alan. I want a word with Kenneth.

**GLENFORSA**

*(With a touch of bitterness!)* As you will then ... It's yours to decide. I'll make a shape at drawing up this deed. My sorrow! I've had experience enough of late to do it as well as any scrivener.

*(Lifting writing-material he goes out R.*

**OSKAMULL**

Elspeth, I'll not be asking how you come to be here, but it's heart sorry I am for the indignities put on you.

**ELSPETH**

Ah! He'll not have told you then why I took Grizel's place?

**OSKAMULL**

Not a word.

**ELSPETH**

It's no matter—no matter. ... I can't help it if you think ill of me. Maybe, indeed, it's best you should.

**OSKAMULL**

Ah! my dear, it's not of you I'll be thinking any ill.

**ELSPETH**

That's kind of you, Kenneth lad.

**OSKAMULL**

*(Hurt.)* Don't. ... I can't bear you to be petting me. It's a man's love I have for you, though you've always made so light of it.

**ELSPETH**

Ah! don't say any more, Kenneth. I'm seeing very plain it's a great wrong I've done you; for you've been the good friend in my trials. I should have told you long ago that I could never be thinking of you as you wished. It's grieved I am, *ille;* but there's no use shutting our eyes to it.

**OSKAMULL**

*(Gloomily.)* It's of Glenforsa you'll be thinking?

**ELSPETH**

With little enough reason, Heaven kens! We have feelings we can't explain to ourselves and can't get by. For good or ill it was fixed for me long ago.

**OSKAMULL**

*(Sullenly, but with kindness.)* What then can I do for you, Elspeth?

Oh! I'm glad to hear you speak that way, Kenneth ... for it's too youthful you are for me. A lad will often be looking to a woman older than himself; but it's not long till he finds out the mistake. *(With a faint smile.)* Why, it's a young lass like Grizel you should have your thoughts on.

**OSKAMULL**

*(Evasively.)* Will I be getting the boat ready?

**ELSPETH**

*(Moving about distractedly.)* Oh, it's home I should be going. And promise me ... promise me, Kenneth—no more drawn swords!

**OSKAMULL**

Why, he's the last man I'd want to harm. It's just he has been the faithful friend to me.

**ELSPETH**

And a minute ago your blades were at each other's breasts. *(Tenderly.)* Weary fa' this hot Highland blood!

**OSKAMULL**

What else would I be doing and him in a temper like yon?

**ELSPETH**

*(Distressed but uplifted.)* Yes, I ken, I ken. He must indeed have been the rude man to you ... But there will be no more of it, ille? Ask him to come in ... There's a good lad! ... I want to see you friends.

*(Oskamull brings Glenforsa back R.*

**GLENFORSA**

*(Entering.)* There's the deed, Kenneth, with the Glenforsa seal and all, used in its own last overthrow! The great Bens are yours ... Ben Talla and the rest ... and they'll not lift their snow-clad peaks a whit less proudly, though bartered away for a dice throw ... I ken you'd prefer to slit my gizzard for them; and I'm not sure but I'd as soon settle it with Sir Claymore myself. And yet ... violence only heaps wrong on wrong.

**ELSPETH**

What is it you've done?

**GLENFORSA**

Gambled away my last stick and acre ... as many a good man has done before me, though maybe with other toys. Now I'm for the foreign wars.

**ELSPETH**

But the estate's an entail!

**GLENFORSA**

Broken ... And sorrow on my father that did it. There's some of my kin might want to dispute this, but they are wandering exiles in stranger lands ... Here's another to their number; and not loath to follow. Since you've small conceit of broken men, Elspeth, I'll not be asking you to come farther with me.

**ELSPETH**

*(Catching her breath.)* It's with a light heart ye go.

**GLENFORSA**

Heavy enough, Guid kens. But I may find a speedy release from it ... Kenneth will see you back to Draolinn.

**ELSPETH**

And what's to come of you—a landless man?

**GLENFORSA**

I've still my sword ... and good friends who'll find employment for it.

**ELSPETH**

I've something I'd like you to wear with your sword, Alan, if you'll be doing it for my sake.

**GLENFORSA**

*(With a laugh.)* Gladly, my dear. You need hardly ask me that.

**ELSPETH**

There then. *(Standing forward.)*

**GLENFORSA**

What is it?

**ELSPETH**

Myself.

**GLENFORSA**

Do you mean that? *(Taking both her hands.)*

**ELSPETH**

*(Laughing to hide her emotion.)* Do you think I don't see what's made you so desperate?

**GLENFORSA**

Elspeth! *M'eudail!* *(Embracing her.)* Ah, but it's nothing now I have to offer you, excepting myself, treasure o' mine!

**ELSPETH**

And what more would I be seeking, *mo chridhe*!

**GLENFORSA**

It will be a trying time for us, my dear. Your father will never forgive.

**ELSPETH**

*(Smiling.)* We'll see ... We'll see.

*(Anna comes in hastily R.*

**ANNA**

*Ochanee, ochanee!* There are two horsemen and a company of gillies coming down the brae-side at Acharonich.
   *(Oskamull goes to window R and pulls aside the window-curtain hangings, showing that it is early morning. The Loch and the distant hills are seen. He looks out to the left.*

**OSKAMULL**

Draolinn!

**ELSPETH**

*(Alarmed)* My father!

*(Anna throws wide the curtains and snuffs out the candles.*

**GLENFORSA**

*(Concerned for Elspeth.)* You could still make your peace with him if I were out of the way.

**ELSPETH**

*(Wistfully)* Then you don't want me?

**GLENFORSA**

More than my life!

**ELSPETH**

Your way, then, is my way.

**GLENFORSA**

But it's of what's best for you I'm thinking.

**OSKAMULL**

*(Lifting deed and throwing it into the fire)* There's what's best for you, Ben This and Ben That.

**ELSPETH**

*(Gratefully)* Kenneth, lad!

**GLENFORSA**

I can't let you do that, Kenneth.

**OSKAMULL**

*(Barring his way.)* I'll not be asking your leave, Alan. You didn't ask mine when you returned my sword. It's time to cry quits.

##### GLENFORSA

*(Feelingly.)* I'm grateful, *laochain* ... and may repay you yet.

> *(The bagpipes are heard at a distance.*

Listen! ... There go the pipes! ... And it's a braggart part they're playing.
" Sons of the dog, come hither and ye shall have flesh."[1]

##### OSKAMULL

*(Listening.)* It's the challenge.

##### GLENFORSA

*(Helping Elspeth with her cloak.)* Your father was aye one for the old
Highland ways. I've little liking to turn my back on a pibroch like yon.

##### ELSPETH

*(Alarmed!)* But, Alan, dear —

##### GLENFORSA

*(With a laugh as he swings on his plaid.)* Oh, I'm not forgetting it's your
father. *(To Oskamull.)* You've the boat ready?

##### OSKAMULL

*(Excitedly.)* Yes. You can get down to the Loch through the postern-gate.

> *(The pipes sound louder.*

##### GLENFORSA

*(Putting on his cap and taking Elspeth's arm.)* Goodbye, lad. And my
compliments to Draolinn. Beannachd leat!

##### OSKAMULL

Beannachd leibh!


**CURTAIN**

## Notes

Overture. " Land of the Mountain and the Flood," by Hamish MacCunn.

As Curtain Rises. " Eriskay Love Lilt," arranged by Kennedy Fraser.

Bagpipes *(in last Scene)*. The marching-tune of Clan Cameron—the clan of old
        Draolinn, Elspeth's father—to be played: *"Pibroch of Donald Dhu"*.
        The air, of course, is to be heard as if from a distance.

Peats may be used before, or on, rise of Curtain, to diffuse aroma of peat
        smoke through theatre for a short period.

Dresses.

Glenforsa: See page 150 of MacIan's *Costumes of the Clans.* Tartan, of course,
        should be a Mackinnon tartan—"hunting tartan" type.

Oskamull: *Ibid.* Page 163. If tartan is worn, MacDougall hunting tartan to be
        used. But, for contrast to Glenforsa, a kilt suit all of crotal of dark
        shade would be best.

Elspeth: Dark costume, not necessarily full riding habit, but one suitable for
        riding— Diana Vernon type. Tricorne hat. Chevelure of Patuffa
        Kennedy Fraser style. A *tonnag*, or small shawl, of Cameron tartan—
        hunting type might be worn, but is not essential.
        For *tonnag*, see *Ibid,* page 195.

Anna: Plain dark dress. *Tonnag* of MacDougall hunting tartan with large
        Celtic brooch.

Tartan and kilt were proscribed by Government at period of the play, but in
outlying districts the law was for long evaded. Exact conformity with details of
dress is therefore not essential. Eighteenth century dress of plain type will be
suitable, but there should be some characteristic Highland details added. If so,
tartan should always conform to clan name of wearer.

## Pronunciation and accent

| | |
|---|---|
| Alan | Al'an. |
| Beannachd leat | Be-yannacht'-laat |
| Beannachd leibh | Be-yannacht'-klyev |
| Ben Talla | Ben Tall'ah |
| Caileag bheag | Kallak vek' |
| Cairn More | Kairnmore' |
| Cruachan | Kroo'achann |
| Draolinn | Dreu'lin (eu like French peu |
| Duart | Doo'-art |
| Elspeth | El'speth |
| Fin M'Coul | Finn Makool' |
| Gaodhail | Gayge'-ull |
| Glenforsa | Glen-for'sa |
| ille! | Ill'y |
| Laochain | Lay'-ochan |
| Loch-na-Keal | Loch-na-Kyall' |
| Mainnir-nam-Fiadh | Mann'yir-nam-Feeah' |
| Mallachd ort | Mallagh orsht' |
| M'eudail | May'-tall |
| Morag | Mor'ag |
| Mo chridhe | Mo-chree' |
| Mo-thruaigh | Mo-roo'ay |
| Och, ochan | Och, och'ann |
| Ochanee | Ochanee' |
| Oskamull | Oss'-kamull |

# The Change-House

Persons of the Play

| | |
|---|---|
| Donnacha MacLean | *Landlord of the Change-House.* |
| Alasdair | *His Gillie.* |
| Iain MacLean | |
| (Iain Dubh) | *Master of the Brig "Margaret."* |
| Flora MacLeod | *Peasant Girl from Innis Fada.* |
| Seonaid | *Her Second Cousin.* |
| Two crofters. | |

TIME 1752.
PLACE   Eilean Aros (Inner Hebrides).
SCENE   The Change-House at Croggan.

*First produced by The Scottish National Players for the St Andrew Society (Glasgow), at the Athenaeum Theatre, Glasgow, on Tuesday, 1st November 1921, with the following cast:*

| | |
|---|---|
| Donnacha | *Mr Donald Robertson* |
| Alasdair | *Mr J. Ronald Young.* |
| Iain Dubh | *Mr R. B. Wharrie.* |
| Flora | *Miss Queenie Russell.* |
| Seonaid | *Miss Jean T. Smith.* |

*The play produced by* Mr Andrew P. Wilson.

SCENE: *Interior of the Change-House at Croggan, late on a September night in 1752. A large, mean, dimly-lit room, half-kitchen, half-drinking chamber. The main door is in the centre of back-wall; and one entering by this has a window in back-wall to right, and a cupboard against back-wall to left. Below window are a spade, some rakes, and a fishing-net; some oars are standing in adjoining corner. In wall to left is a rude hollow, serving for fire-place. Peats are aglow in this; and two lit cruisies hang from either end of the mantel-shelf. Nearer back, in same wall, is a door leading to back of house. In wall to right, about midway, is a door leading to the sleeping chambers. In the centre of room are two tables and a bench. On the tables are drink-vessels — tappit-hens in pewter, some wood-ware, and such like. On either side the fire is a plain, rudely-fashioned chair.*

*The night is wild, and the coarse curtain over the window flaps occasionally as the squalls break over the building.* THE LANDLORD, *a big strong man of sixty, in peasant dress, is making a pretence of clearing tables and setting room in order. He is doing practically nothing, fidgetting and loafing by turns; his mind evidently preoccupied by something else than the business in hand.*

ALASDAIR, *his gillie, a somewhat vacant-faced lad of eighteen, is, however, really working hard at same task; but, after a space, goes to window, and peers out.*

LANDLORD

Will you be leaving that window, and getting on wi' your work?
(ALASDAIR *resumes clearing table, but is evidently both amused and perplexed at being ordered about by one who is idling.*

ALASDAIR

It's well the people crossed before the storm began. The wind's rising. The loch's white wi' scud.

LANDLORD

(*Bitterly.*) Aye! The Croggan folk were aye keen on a hanging. A night in the wet heather's nothing to them, if they'll can see a pretty man at the end o' a tow in the morning.

ALASDAIR

Poor Callum! What time will they do't, think you?

LANDLORD

About ten, I'm hearing.
(ALASDAIR *is drawn to window again.*

ALASDAIR

The moon —

LANDLORD

Will you get on wi' your work, *amadan*!

**ALASDAIR**

*(Coming back from window.)* 'Save us, the moon's broke through! I can see the gibbet, now ... plain on the hill-top it is!

**LANDLORD**

Wheesht you wi' your gibbets! My heart's sore enough for Callum already, without your harping on't. Get you to your work, *ille*.

**ALASDAIR**

*(Resuming tidying, but still amazed at the contrast between his own industry and the other's idleness.)* Rob More was saying he was on Maol Ban this evening, and he was seeing Iain Dubh's brig in the Lynn o' Lorne.

**LANDLORD**

Iain Dubh back! Are ye sure, lad?

**ALASDAIR**

Rob's no' likely to mistake. He was in her crew at one time.

**LANDLORD**

Iain Dubh back! And his own cousin to die a dule-tree death the morn at Gualachaolish! I had rather than fifty pund Iain didna land for a week to come!

**ALASDAIR**

He'll never can land if the storm gets worse.

**LANDLORD**

Will he no'? Ye dinna ken Iain, I'm thinking. *(Then horror-struck.)* My sorrow! What will be the end o' this! Iain back!

**ALASDAIR**

*(At window again.)* The tide's high the night. We'll need to be pulling up the boats.

**LANDLORD**

Will you be keeping to your work? All the same I'd best be taking a look at the boats. It will indeed be the high tide this night wi' that wind.
*(He goes out by back-door. alasdair sets to dusting tables clumsily. A knock is heard at main-door, and a voice singing "The Sea-Reivers." Door opens and* **IAIN MACLEAN** (**IAIN DUBH**) *enters, still singing. He finishes his verse with a swaggering roll of his body, claps alasdair on the shoulder, and shakes hands with him.*
*iain Dubh is a man of thirty-five. He has a dark, flashing eye, and dark curly hair. His manner is restrained in order to conceal a nature impulsive and candid. His dress is of rough seafaring type.*

**IAIN**

Well, Alasdair, there ye are, busy wi' the ale-stoups as usual. Be getting me some of the good stuff, *ille*.

**ALASDAIR**

(*Going out at back-door and returning with drinking-vessels.*) It's you after all, Captain. Rob More saw the brig from Maol Ban the day, but the master wasna for believing it could be you.

**IAIN**

And what for no'? It's four months since I left, and time I was home to this good ale, lad. Nothing like it in Holland, I'll assure you. *Slainte mhath!* (*He drinks.*) And what now, will you tell me, are all the watch-fires doing across the Sound at Gualachaolish?

**ALASDAIR**

The people crossed to-night, fearing the storm would keep them from crossing in the morning.

**IAIN**

They'd good cause for their fears, I'm thinking. If the wind gets to the North 'twill be the big storm. But what's ado over there? A wedding at the marriage-tree at Killean?

**ALASDAIR**

A wedding! Have you no' heard? (*Goes to window.*) Aye ... there's the moon now. Look!

**IAIN**

What is't, *ille*?

**ALASDAIR**

Yon—on the hill.

**IAIN**

Mary Mother! A gibbet! What's afoot, lad? Who is't?

**ALASDAIR**

Callum o' Strathcoil.

**IAIN**

Callum?

**ALASDAIR**

Aye. Ye've been four months away. Ye wadna hear o't.

**IAIN**

(*Breathlessly.*) What was it?

He shot a sodger in Glenlussa, and the sodger died on them.

**IAIN**

God above!

*(The Landlord enters, Iain grasps his hand warmly.*
Is this true, Donnacha? Did the red-coat die after the ploy in the Glen?
And is Callum to swing for't!

**LANDLORD**

*(To alasdair.)* Be getting Rob More to help you pull up the boats.

*(***ALASDAIR*** goes out.*
*(To iain, gravely.)* I see you have it, Iain. It's owre true.

**IAIN**

Donnacha, Donnacha! here is the black day! It was my hand fired yon
shot.

**LANDLORD**

*(Gently.)* It's what I was aye thinking, Iain.

**IAIN**

*(Distractedly.)* Callum was wi' me in the wood; but he had no hand in it,
I tell you! I but meant to wing the fellow for his insolence. My sorrow! I
kent the man was ill, but he showed no sign o' dying when I sailed.

**LANDLORD**

He died a week after.

**IAIN**

Donnacha, Donnacha! Callum maunna die that gate. How many red-
coats are there in the garrison?

**LANDLORD**

Sixty or thereby.

**IAIN**

That'll mean forty at the gibbet. We'll can do't! God! that it may rain in
torrents the morn!

**LANDLORD**

For why?

**IAIN**

To soak their powder-horns well, *ille!*

**LANDLORD**

You'll never be thinking of a lifting, Iain!

**IAIN**

What else, man! Aye, from the gibbet-foot itself, if need be.

**LANDLORD**

Iain, Iain, bethink you!

**IAIN**

I've twenty men on the brig; and the Croggan lads will surely no' be backward to help. We can count on fifty in all, I'm thinking. You've some arms here?

**LANDLORD**

You'll never do't. It's too desperate a stroke.

**IAIN**

Maybe. But it's Callum we're fighting for. We'll get them near the water's edge. I'll have the boats handy; and we'll have him on the brig like the hawk, and it swooping, man!

**LANDLORD**

The hawk leaves blood on the heather at times, Iain.

**IAIN**

And what though? Anything rather than Callum dying the halter-death.

**LANDLORD**

And that's true. But—the brig —?

**IAIN**

The brig's standing off and on for me all night.

**LANDLORD**

It's the rough sea. And if the wind goes full North —

**IAIN**

Man, you daunt me there! But we've the rough lads for the rough sea. We've seen Corrievrecken afore now. All the same, you're right, Donnacha. *(Biting his finger-nails.)* If it comes full North, she'll have to run for Kerrera and shelter there. And then where are we?

**LANDLORD**

We're by wi't then, I'm fearing.

**IAIN**

No, nor by wi't. We maun lippen on Croggan lads at that rate. Are there any here who havena crossed?

**LANDLORD**

Kenandroma and Portmore.

**IAIN**

I'll make sure o' them then, brig or no brig.

*(He goes swiftly to the door.*

Be you looking to your arms, Donnacha.

*(HE goes out; and the LANDLORD going to aumry takes out some arms parcelled in cloths, and, unwrapping them, lays them on table. He is examining these, when a knock comes to the door. He wraps up arms again hurriedly, and replaces them. FLORA and SEONAID MACLEOD enter. FLORA is a fair-haired girl; her mien is gentle and drooping. The other—her second cousin—SEONAID, is a bright-eyed, dark-haired lass, with something of brusquerie, and more of confidence, in her bearing. Both are travel-stained and weary. They remove their plaids, and drop the portion of their arisaids which they are wearing as hoods, as they come in.*

**FLORA**

A stormy night, goodman of the house. Is this the Inns?

**LANDLORD**

By your leave, my lass, not much of an Inns, only a poor kind of a change-house. We've little comfort for folk wanting to rest overnight. Is it far you'll have come?

**FLORA**

From Innis Fada.

**LANDLORD**

'Shield us! What a journey! And would you not now be trying the Widow MacKinnon's? .... the first house —

**SEONAID**

Goodman, is it Gael you are? We are ill with the great weariness. Can we no' be stopping here?

*(FLORA, almost fainting, has sat down suddenly, her head in her hands.*

**LANDLORD**

*(Regarding flora.)* Well, well! your will to you. It is indeed a long journey. My chamber is none of the best, look you. *(To SEONAID.)* Take you the cruisie, and I'll help this weary one.

*(HE assists FLORA to rise, and they go out by door on right. The LANDLORD returns, and speaking over his shoulder, says:*

I'll be getting you a bite and a sup o' kail.

*(HE busies himself at fire and at cupboard with dishes. SEONAID returns, and sits down by fire. Landlord stirs kail-pot.*

**SEONAID**

It's cold I am. She's lying down for a bit.

**LANDLORD**

Aye, a long journey that. And where now did you land, I wonder?

**SEONAID**

At Carsaig. We're for Duart. But there was a thick mist at Kinlochspelvie, and we missed our way.

**LANDLORD**

You'll have friends at Duart?

**SEONAID**

Aye, a brother o' this one.

**LANDLORD**

Well, well! "Bare is shoulder without brother", as the saying is.
        (**SEONAID** *makes a startled movement, and catches her breath.*
And she'll be kin to you, the lass ben?

**SEONAID**

A second cousin, goodman.

**LANDLORD**

So? It'll be a long time now, since you left Innis Fada?

**SEONAID**

A day and a night in the boat, and a day tramping the heather here.

**LANDLORD**

A long time that. I wonder now, will I be kenning the lad you're seeking?

**SEONAID**

(*Bitterly.*) You'll ken his name at least well enough. He was Seoras MacLeod, the sodger killed by the man that's to hang the morn.

**LANDLORD**

My pain and my longing! Is this the lad's sister?

**SEONAID**

(*Listlessly.*) Aye, but she ken's nothing o' his death as yet. She thinks him only deadly ill.

**LANDLORD**

*Och, ochan!*

**SEONAID**

Myself, I heard the truth but an hour back. A waif word from an auld wife by the roadside set me speiring.

**LANDLORD**

And you've said nocht to the lass?

**SEONAID**

I hadna the heart.

**LANDLORD**

This night, this night!

**SEONAID**

Was he long ill of his wound?

**LANDLORD**

Six days.

**SEONAID**

We only got his message, a poor shaky scrape it was, and no date on't, four days ago.

**LANDLORD**

It's taken months to reach you, has it?

**SEONAID**

Aye. It's a long road to Innis Fada when there's writing to do. It maun have miscarried, gone round by Kintail and Skye, I'm thinking.

**LANDLORD**

Poor lass!

**SEONAID**

*Ochanoch!* It will kill her when she hears.

**LANDLORD**

Poor lass! (**He** *moves restlessly about, and at last goes to window.*) The moon's clear again. You maun keep her from seeing yon. It will set her to the asking of questions.

**SEONAID**

(*Joining him at window.*) The gallows! I didna ken it was to be here.

**LANDLORD**

Aye, just here. Poor Callum!

**SEONAID**

Callum?

**LANDLORD**

The lad that's to die the morn.

**SEONAID**

And you can be pitying him? Myself, I'm glad to see that gibbet, glad, glad!

**LANDLORD**

I'm no' so sure 'twas Callum's hand that fired the shot, look you. The trial at Inneraora was none too fair.

**SEONAID**

Of course, of course! You'll be of the same tartan as Callum, I'm thinking?

**LANDLORD**

Aye, and not 'shamed o't either.

**SEONAID**

And not 'shamed! I was thinking that would be the way o't! MacLeans! Unfriends to the King and a' that's kindly!

**LANDLORD**

And where's your King?

**SEONAID**

(*Evasively, as she controls her anger*) Will I be taking up a sup to the lass?

**LANDLORD**

(*Muttering.*) MacLeods! MacLeods! (*Then in his usual tone.*) Indeed, yes. (*He fills a bowl with kail.*) But you'll no' be telling her this night?

**SEONAID**

She'll hear nothing from me till we're close on Duart the morn. His grave will be there?

**LANDLORD**

Aye, nearby the Castle. Had ye no other friends in the Isle?

**SEONAID**

Only an acquaintance. A shipmaster. He came from hereabouts, and sailed our way sometimes. A MacLean he was. Iain Dubh by name.

**LANDLORD**

God shield us!

**SEONAID**

What's amiss, goodman? You ken him?

**LANDLORD**

Aye, I ken him. But he's from home, look you. Sailing the high seas he is. Yes. That's what he's at, yes; sailing the deep seas. Yes, yes. He's from home is Iain.

**SEONAID**

You're the strange man.

**LANDLORD**

I am that. And these are the strange times, let me tell you.

**SEONAID**

Wheesht! I hear Flora stirring. She may be coming down. You'll let nothing slip your tongue about Seoras's death.

**LANDLORD**

Is it me? No, no. I'll be going, for I was ever the poor hand at hiding my own mind. Be saying to her that I've gone down to draw up the boats, will you?

(**He** *goes out; and after a little* **FLORA** *enters and sits down by the fire.*

**FLORA**

I'm shivering. It's fine to see a fire. Where's the goodman? Did he have any word of Seoras?

**SEONAID**

What word would he have? The folks hereabouts are no' like our own people; they've no dealings wi' the soldiers.

**FLORA**

Poor Seoras! Was there no word of a plague in the countryside? I'm wondering if it was the plague that was in it with Seoras.

**SEONAID**

*(Filling bowls with soup from pot, and bringing scones from cupboard.)* Let your mind be at ease; for it's to-morrow we'll be at Duart. Say your grace now, and take a sup and bite, for it's long fasting you are.

(*They bend their heads in silent prayer, and then make a simple meal. The wind moans around the house. A step is heard on the gravel.*

**FLORA**

There's the goodman's foot. I maun try him about Seoras. Maybe he'll be more open wi' me.

(*Knock at door, and* **IAIN DUBH** *enters.*

**IAIN**

Your pardon. Is himself at home? What! And is it Flora of Valtos, and Seonaid too? It's a far cry to Erisort! *(To* **FLORA***.)* Whatever are you making of it here, lass?

(*Both girls have risen in surprise.* **FLORA** *is blushing. She goes to* **IAIN** *and weeps on his breast.*

**FLORA**

Och, Iain, Iain! but it's me that's glad to see you!

**IAIN**

You're ill, lass?

**FLORA**

Tired, tired. We've been long journeying.

**IAIN**

Sit you down now, for you're trembling, and as white's the *canach*. And what brings you to my calf-country?

(**FLORA** *weeps silently.*

**SEONAID**

She'll no' can tell you. We had word from her brother, Seoras, the first word since he ran away from home three years ago. We were to come to Duart. He was a sodger and lay deadly ill there.

**FLORA**

Is there plague in the garrison, Iain? Oh, I hope it will no' be plague.

**IAIN**

Plague! It might well be in a stack o' black stones like yon barracks. But I ken naught o' the countryside's news as yet. I'm but half an hour landed. You must ask the goodman.

**FLORA**

You've been sailing the wide world, Iain, I'm thinking, for it's little we've heard of you in Erisort this year and more.

**IAIN**

(With meaning.) I ken what you're thinking, lass. Aye. Dunkerque, Havre, and the Baltic, many trips, and four months on this last. But it's sorry I am to hear of the poor lad, Flora. And yet—

**FLORA**

Yes?

**IAIN**

And yet a sodger like him'll be better in his bed the morn than out o't.

**FLORA**

For why?

**IAIN**

There's trouble in the countryside these days.

**FLORA**

What is't, Iain, this trouble?

**IAIN**

Don't ask me, lass. (He sinks his face to his hands, then looks up, smiling.) Och, but let us no' be thinking o't! It's yourself that's here, and that's the great matter.

**FLORA**

Iain, Iain! You've the great sorrow on you! What's amiss?

**IAIN**

I canna tell a' my mind, lass. Let's leave it there.

**FLORA**

It's the sore trouble, I'm seeing.

**IAIN**

It'll be gone then before the sun sets again, lass. I'll win through't.
Never fear!

**FLORA**

And you'll can take me to Duart the morn?

**IAIN**

No' for a day or two, Flora. You maunna move out o' this till the
trouble's over.

**FLORA**

My sorrow! To be so near Seoras, and to wait and wait!

**SEONAID**

(*Hurriedly.*) Wheesht you, lass! Iain kens best.

**IAIN**

Where's the goodman?

**SEONAID**

Down beaching the skiffs.

**FLORA**

Maybe you'll be getting more out o' him than incomers like Seonaid
and myself—about Seoras, I mean. We'll wait up for him now you're
here.

**SEONAID**

(*Alarmed lest the truth come out.*) Indeed then, and I think you're no'
wise, Flora, and you dead tired. Myself, I'm worn out, and it's lying
down I'll be. *Oidhche mhath*, Iain.

**IAIN**

*Oidhche mhath*, Seonaid.

(**SEONAID** *shakes hands with him and goes out.*)
Come now, Flora, you'll no' be mourning for Seoras. If it's plague that's
in it, he'll be up and about in two weeks' time or less.

**FLORA**

Aye, if he comes through.

**IAIN**

He'll be no brother o' yours if he doesna. Healthy as the deer, he should
be a Valtos man.

**FLORA**

I'm fearing.

**IAIN**

And some fine day soon we'll cross to Gualachaolish, and take through the hill to Duart. 'Tis there is the fine country, Flora, when the sun's out and shining bravely. You'll think yourself in Innis Fada again!

**FLORA**

You're sure you've the good hope of him, Iain?

**IAIN**

I'm sure, lass. And we'll be putting the mountain-moor under our feet; and we'll be together again. Think you o' that!

**FLORA**

Oh, Iain!

**IAIN**

And round us the lambs bleating, and the happy folk at the *cas-chrom* or the peats!

**FLORA**

Like Innis Fada!

**IAIN**

Finer than Erisort itself is that same country! *(Then softly.)* But I'll be taking that back, for Erisort will ever be the dearest o' memories to me. The shieling above Keose, lass, eh?

**FLORA**

*(Smiling.)* I mind it well, Iain.

**IAIN**

White love! and can I be forgetting?

**FLORA**

*(Disengaging the hand which he has taken.)* But I mind too that you went off without the goodbye to me or any o' mine, Iain MacLean. I'm fearing you're the light-hearted one.

**IAIN**

Be you fair now, Flora! I had a hunted man to run to France. It was life or death, up anchor and go, never a moment to spare.

**FLORA**

You might well have sent some wee word at least to Flora MacLeod.

**IAIN**

I could send no word with safety, lass. Tearlach Og's is a hard service, you ken. But often I was for Erisort since then, yet aye failed till this run. Once I had cleared my business here, I was straight for Innis Fada.

*(Mockingly.)* You tell me!

IAIN

It's fifteen months since I've seen you, my dear; and have not I been wearying sore?

FLORA

You aye had the soft tongue, Iain.

IAIN

*Mo chridhe!* It's truth I'm giving you.

FLORA

*(Suddenly reminiscent.)* Oh, Iain! Do you mind when we first met! The wee lamb in the blackboyd bush, and me slashing away to set it free?

IAIN

And me, not knowing you were there, slashing away from the other side, and meeting you in the heart o' the thicket? 'Twas the droll ploy!

FLORA

'Twas the bonnie lamb, yon!

IAIN

Mary Mother! And did not I get there the start! Seeing the finest face in all the world and it bleeding among the thorns!

FLORA

Scartit face or no', 'twas me was the first to get to the lamb.

IAIN

Indeed and you didn't then, Flora, for 'twas myself that put him in your arms.

FLORA

*(Irritably.)* Och! Maybe I was not there at all then! *(Then smiling radiantly.)* But, oh! wasn't he the wee darling?

IAIN

And wasn't he the ungrateful one, all the same? Never a *baa* by way of a thank-ye, but off to the old ewe in a scamper.

FLORA

Indeed and you're wrong now. For I thought he said something to me when I kissed his nose in the bush yonder.

IAIN

You only thought he did. I wouldna have so failed you, had you been as kindly to me.

#### FLORA

Now, aren't you the brazen one, Iain MacLean?

#### IAIN

The wooden one more like, that I hadna the sense to profit by that bush o' brambles, and you fast held in it.

#### FLORA

What a man to rave!

#### IAIN

If only I'd been gleg enough!

#### FLORA

*(Rising.)* I think I'll be going.

#### IAIN

No, nor going. *(His arm steals round her.)* Listen, white love! Fifteen months is a long time, and here at last is the day I've been wearying for. You'll no' be going, will you?

#### FLORA

Iain Dubh, but you've the sweet tongue. *(They kiss.)* Wheesht! There's the goodman's foot. I'd best be going. *Oidhche mhath, mo chridhe!*

#### IAIN

*Oidhche mhath!* 'Sweet sleep to you, my dear one!
    (**FLORA** *goes out by door on right. After a moment the* **LANDLORD** *enters by main-door.*
I made nothing o' Kenandroma or Portmore, Donnacha. They're the white-livered lot. They'll no' move the morn unless the men from the brig are in the fight.
    (*The* **LANDLORD** *marches up and down the room in gloomy meditation, unheeding Iain.*
What's come to you, Donnacha?

#### LANDLORD

The last curse, I'm thinking. *(He crosses to the door of the girls' chamber and listens there.)* His sister's here.

#### IAIN

Whose sister?

#### LANDLORD

The sister of Seoras MacLeod, the red-coat that was shot in Glenlussa.

#### IAIN

*Mo thruaighe!* *(He rises, bewildered as the truth dawns on him.)* Oh, Flora! Flora! *(He stumbles towards the door, and rushes out into the dark.)*
    (*At the outcry* **FLORA** *and* **SEONAID** *appear at the door of their room.*

Someone called, goodman.

**LANDLORD**

*(Distracted, shaking his fist savagely.)* MacLeods! MacLeods! Get you gone from under my roof; for it's the black destruction you've brought on Croggan! MacLeods! MacLeods!

> **(He** *goes out hastily after* **IAIN**.

**FLORA**

I'm sure I heard my name cried out.

**SEONAID**

I wonder now.

**FLORA**

*(Looking from window.)* Oh! see, Seonaid! see! The moon's out, and there's a gallows-tree on the hill over. It's the wild country this!

> **(SEONAID** *buries her face in her hands.*

What is't, Seonaid? You're hiding something from me, woman! I've felt it all night. What is't? Oh! it canna be! It canna be!

**SEONAID**

Wheesht, Flora, wheesht!

**FLORA**

It's no' for Seoras—yon? It wasna because o' yon he sent us word?

**SEONAID**

No, no, be thankit! But, my grief! My grief! It's killed he is, and yon's the gibbet for his slayer!

**FLORA**

*(Weeping.)* Ochonarie! Ochonarie!

**SEONAID**

Wheesht you, lass! Wheesht! Here's this wild landlord back again.

> *(The* **LANDLORD** *appears, leading iain dazed and distraught.* **IAIN** *signs by a finger on his lips that the* **LANDLORD** *is to keep silence.* **FLORA** *flies to iain, and sinks weeping on his breast.*

**IAIN**

Be leaving us, Donnacha. Seonaid.

> **(SEONAID** *goes out by door on right; the* **LANDLORD** *by door on left.*

**FLORA**

Oh, Iain, you've heard? Seoras is killed on us.

**IAIN**

*(Brokenly)* Aye, lass. I've heard. I never dreamt—

**FLORA**

*Ochonarie!*

**IAIN**

*(Comforting her.)* My dear! My dear!

**FLORA**

And now it's you are for some wild ploy the morn! And who kens, who kens, but you'll be lost on us also. You'll no' be going, Iain. You'll no' be going!

**IAIN**

My dear lass!

**FLORA**

Ah! you'll go; and you'll be lost on us as well as Seoras!

**IAIN**

I maun go.

**FLORA**

For why?

**IAIN**

To save a man that's innocent o' your brother's death, Flora.

**FLORA**

*(Going to window, and shrinking back from what she sees on the hill-top.)* Oh! Is't that? Iain, Iain!

**IAIN**

My poor lass!

**FLORA**

Och! Seoras! Seoras! Oh! the black day. And what's to come to Flora MacLeod, wi' brother gone and lover gone? You'll no' do't, Iain? Iain?

**IAIN**

I canna let Callum die that gate.

**FLORA**

You'll never come back, I'm fearing. And then it's alone I'll be, alone, alone!

**IAIN**

My lass, my lass!

**FLORA**

Oh! it's home I'd be, home, home, in Erisort.

#### IAIN

Aye, and it's home you'll be, before long, Flora, dear, and it's the morn you'll sail too. The brig's no' slow, lass! And it's soon you'll be home again. Poor Seoras! I'd give my right hand —

#### FLORA

Seoras! Seoras! Home! Home!

#### IAIN

My dear, my dear! Be you grieving your fill, for it's the sore trial. But it's in Erisort you'll be before two days are over. And some night of the clear moon we'll be going up to the old shieling again, you and me, and thinking o' the poor lad that's gone, and —

#### FLORA

Seoras! Seoras!

#### IAIN

And we'll be seeing the loch like silver below us, and we'll be threading the old paths in the black gullies —

#### FLORA

Aye, aye! But the morn, Iain, the ploy the morn!

#### IAIN

Tach! It's but a little thing that! I'll win through, lass, I tell you.

#### FLORA

He didna do't, you say, this Callum?

#### IAIN

No.

#### FLORA

And who then? (*Now firily.*) Can you no' be laying your hands on the right man, and be done wi't without further bloodshed? It's killed you'll be, Iain!

#### IAIN

I think I ken the right man.

#### FLORA

(*Joyfully.*) And you're for seizing him the morn? Oh! gang to your ploy then, and a blessing wi' you! Bring him to the halter, and save your friend!

#### IAIN

My dear, my dear! Oh! what is't you're saying now! The man who slew your brother had no mind to do that same. He'd no desire of his death, Flora lass.

**FLORA**

And what now? Oh, Seoras! Seoras! Is it to this it's come? You'd few friends in life, lad, and none in death. You're slain, and all I get is words and words and words. Your blood cries out, and there's none will answer.

**IAIN**

*(In anguish.)* Flora! Flora!

**FLORA**

Take not my name on your lips, Iain Dubh, if it's thus you're to fail me. There are men in Erisort still, be thankit! and some o' them'll be in Duart before long, once I tell them my story.

**IAIN**

Flora, lass! *(He sinks to a chair, his head in his hands.)*

**FLORA**

What is't I'm saying! Iain, Iain! you've the great sorrow. My words are wild, and I'm not for seeing my way clear. I'm not for understanding this at all, at all.

**IAIN**

You're hard, lass, you're hard!

**FLORA**

*Mo thruaighe!* I've hurt you sore, Iain. Have pity on poor Flora! Her mind's not her own. Iain! Iain! Oh! to be back in Erisort wi' you, and forgetting all this blackness!

**IAIN**

Erisort? I wonder, will it ever be?

**FLORA**

Think you on Erisort, my man, for it's there we were happy. And now I'm seeing you've the trouble on you that's greater than mine, my love. Oh! your eyes so wild! *Mo chridhe!*

**IAIN**

I'm seeing it. I'm seeing it!

**FLORA**

*(Terrified and clinging to him.)* Is it the sight is on you, Iain?

**IAIN**

*(Coming to himself as if from a trance.)* I dinna ken, lass; but it was naught evil. 'Twas the old shieling above Keose, lass. *(His face becomes serene again.)* Aye, we'll be going there, Flora, when this dark day's but a memory that's faded. It will be moonlight there. And your face will be

like the white moss, shining and shining in the night, my love, and the scent o' your hair finer than the bog-myrtle, and your words lovelier than the wee burns tinkling in the dark.

**FLORA**

Iain, Iain!

**IAIN**

And the snipe and the curlew will cry about us in the hill yonder. And down by the shore Keose will show a lit window or maybe two. And the Catechist's dog will be barking far below; and there will be a wee murmur o' talk floating up from the fishers at Cromore. And Flora MacLeod will be high on the hill above, her cheek on the bell-heather; but she'll no' be minding the roughness o' that pillow at all, for Iain Dubh, her lover, will be sharing it with her.

**FLORA**

*Mo chridhe!*

**IAIN**

And it's oh! on that hill will be all the dark beauty o' the night, the stars burning, and the moon beaming, and your face the bonniest of all the things there, my dear!

**FLORA**

*(Yielding herself to his passionate embrace.) Mo chridhe!*

**IAIN**

*Mo thruaighe!* My lass, it's the strange world! But let us be keeping the stout hearts. This life's indeed the steep hill; but the day's long, and we'll be at the top yet.

**FLORA**

I'll be going now, Iain.

**IAIN**

Go you if you will, my dear. You're worn out.

**FLORA**

*Oidhche mhath*, Iain. *(She kisses him.)*

**IAIN**

*Oidhche mhath, m'eudail!*
      (**SHE** *goes out wearily; and* **HE** *sits down by fire to brood, gnawing at his finger-nails.* **HE** *goes to window and looks out anxiously at sky. The wind is heard rising a little. The* **LANDLORD** *enters with* alasdair.)

**LANDLORD**

I've been up on Maol Ben—

#### IAIN

The brig?

#### LANDLORD

The wind's full North—a gale. She's heading for shelter behind Kerrera.

#### IAIN

(*With a despairing toss of his hands.*) Here's the end o' the rescue then.

#### LANDLORD

Aye, ye've lost the help o' twenty stout men wi' that wind, lad. Be thinking better o't.

#### IAIN

These cowards at Kenandroma and Portmore! The rest over there will be o' the same mind! We're done, Donnacha!

#### LANDLORD

Aye, we're done, Iain.

#### IAIN

(*After a moments gloomy meditation.*) I'll put a stop on this, though. I'm for Duart. Out wi' a boat, Alasdair!

#### LANDLORD

Man, man! What is't you're for doing?

#### IAIN

I'm for the Major at Duart, I tell ye! If any's to hang, it maunna be poor Callum!

#### LANDLORD

Bethink you, lad! They'll hang ye both. Aye, and so wad they every MacLean in the Isle, if they dared.

#### IAIN

Out, Alasdair, out! I'm for crossing the loch!

#### LANDLORD

You'll launch the skiff yourself then, and that you'll never do in a storm like this! Man! the squalls are coming off Craigaven like whooping devils, the 'och's foaming like a witch's pot.

#### IAIN

It's round by the head o' the Loch I'll be going then, Donnacha, even if I've to crawl on hands and knees. I'm for Duart this very night.

#### LANDLORD

You're flinging away your life, Iain MacLean; for Callum's doomed, whatever!

**IAIN**

Stop you! Rob More has a garron! I'll do't riding!

*(He dashes out into the night.*

**LANDLORD**

Cry up Portmore, Alasdair! Cry up Kenandroma! Haste ye! Tell them your story. Say that Iain Dubh's flinging away his life! I'll up to Rob's after him. Even if I've to hamstring his horse, he maun never make Duart!

*(ALASDAIR stumbles out noisily. The clamour brings FLORA and SEONAID on the scene. They are in a state of alarm and disarray. Both wear short plaids on their shoulders.*

**FLORA**

What's all the outcry for, goodman?

**LANDLORD**

MacLeods! MacLeods! Spawn o' traitors! Woe worth the day I ever set eyes on ye! MacLeods!

*(He rummages in the aumry, seizes a rope and runs out into the wind and rain.*

**FLORA**

Whatever has come over him at all, at all!

**SEONAID**

I wonder what will it be?

**FLORA**

Wheesht you! I hear Iain's voice out there. Oh! *mo thruaighe!* What a world!

*(She goes to open door and peers out into the dark.*
I hear him! Iain! Iain! Where are ye, my man? my man?

**SEONAID**

He's coming. I hear them. Yonder!

*(THEY draw back as a posse of men enter with IAIN DUBH in their midst. TWO CROFTERS hold him; and his arms are bound to his side by a rope. The LANDLORD and ALASDAIR are in front of him. FLORA brushes them aside, and goes to IAIN.*

**FLORA**

*(Beseechingly.)* What's this of it, Iain! What's come to you at all, at all?

**IAIN**

It's the good-bye, lass. You and I maun twine.

**LANDLORD**

*(Whispering to IAIN.)* Wheesht you about yon, lad!

#### IAIN

*(Disregarding him.)* I tell't ye they had the wrong man for the gibbet, Flora. And that's true. 'Twas my hand held the black gun o' misfortune, and it's me should be in Callum's shoes the morn.

#### LANDLORD

Wheesht you, lad!

#### IAIN

*(Savagely.)* Ay, and it's there I'd be too, but for these meddlesome fools. God! But I'll make them rue it yet!

#### FLORA

Oh, Iain lad! And was it you!

#### SEONAID

*(Picking up table-knife and dashing at* IAIN.*)* Scum o' the pit! Is't death you're seeking, Iain Dubh?
  *(***FLORA**, *who is nearest, grasps her hand, disarms her, and tosses knife in fire.*
                    SEONAID *crouches away from her in remorse.*

#### FLORA

Isn't there pain and sorrow enough in the world?
                    *(The* **LANDLORD** *whispers to* **FLORA**.
Yes, yes, goodman, be taking him away to a safe place! What for should two men die the morn instead o' one!

#### IAIN

*(Bitterly.)* Aye! be taking me from this. For it's not one roof that should be covering her head and mine any more. Oh, *mo chridhe! mo chridhe!*

#### LANDLORD

Out for the shieling at Garmonyreoch, lads!
  *(***THEY** *pass out slowly into the night with their prisoner. As* IAIN *crosses the threshold,* **FLORA**, *with a grave protective gesture, takes off her plaid, and places it on his shoulders.*

#### FLORA

Fare you well, my love, and forever!
                    *(Then, turning to* **SEONAID**, *she falls weeping on her breast.*
Oh! Seonaid, Seonaid!

#### CURTAIN

# Pronunciation

| | |
|---|---|
| Amadan | A'matan |
| Dubh | Doo |
| Gualachaolish | Goolachoolish |
| ille | Illy |
| Innis Fada | Innish Fa'ta |
| Keose | Kyosé |
| M'eudail. | May'tal |
| Mo thruaighe | Moroo'ay |
| Mo chridhe | Mochree' |
| Oidhche mhath | O'eechyva' |
| Seonaid . | Shon'atj |
| Seoras | Sho'rass |
| Strathcoil . | Strachool' |
| Tearlach Og | Cherrlach Oke' |

'

# Notes

OVERTURE.—"Prelude to the 'Change-House' " by J. Seymour Halley.

BEFORE CURTAIN RISES.—" An Island Sheiling Song" (violin solo), from " Songs of the Hebrides" arranged by Kennedy Fraser.

PEATS.—May be used before, or on, rise of curtain to diffuse aroma of peat smoke through theatre for a short period.

COSTUMES.—No tartan or kilt should be worn, as the district of the play is under military occupation, and both were proscribed by Government at period of play.

FLORA AND SEONAID.—See pages 123 and 203 of MacIan's *Costumes of the Clans* for arisaids, etc.

IAIN DUBH, DONNACHA, AND ALASDAIR—Lowland peasant dress of the period.

# Rory Aforesaid

A Comedy in One Act

Founded on *Maistre Pierre Pathelin,* an old French Play
—15th Century—of unknown authorship.

## Persons

| | |
|---|---|
| MacConnachie | *Sheriff-COURT OFFICER.* |
| Mr. MacCallum | *Merchant and Tenant of a small sheep-farm.* |
| Rory MacColl | *Shepherd to Mr. MacCallum.* |
| Mr. MacIntosh | *Lawyer from Oban.* |
| The **she**riff-Substitute | *Also from Oban.* |
| Mrs. MacLean | *Crofter Woman.* |

THE TIME is the present. A day in October.
THE PLACE is the little town of Torlochan in the West Highlands.

*RORY AFORESAID was produced by the Scottish National Theatre Society, at the Lyric Theatre, Glasgow, on 21st October, 1926, under the direction of Tyrone Guthrie, with the following cast:*

| | |
|---|---|
| The court officer | *Andrew Stewart.* |
| MacCallum | *John Rae.* |
| Rory | *Archie Buchanan.* |
| Macintosh | *G. Paterson Whyte.* |
| The sheriff | *J. H. N. Craigen.* |
| Mrs. MacLean | *Elliot C. Mason.* |

*Scene.*— *The Sheriff-Court at Torlochan: a large chamber with whitewashed walls, panelled in lower part with yellow pine. Two tall gaunt windows are in the back wall. In the left wall, near the back, is a door, leading to the* SHERIFF'S *retiring-room. In the right wall, towards the front, is another door, an entrance for the public. To the left is the* SHERIFF'S *desk on a low platform; a table for his clerk is at the side of it. In the centre of the floor-space is the table for solicitors, with chairs around it. Between the table and the* SHERIFF'S *desk, but somewhat towards the back, is the witness-stand. To the right are benches for the public.*

DUNCAN MACCALLUM, *merchant and sheep-farmer from Ardnish, is walking up and down the empty chamber to keep himself warm, for there is an October chill in the air. He is an erect old man of sixty, with grizzled hair and beard. He wears a square-topped hat, and a muffler is wound over the collar of his stout overcoat. To him there enters the* COURT OFFICER, *a man of fifty, with his few remaining dark hairs carefully combed in separate lines across the bald portion of his scalp. He wears a black tie, and his square-cut coat has an official look.*

#### COURT OFFICER
Will you not be coming in to the fire in the waiting-room, Mr. MACCALLUM? It's cold in this big tomb of a place.

#### MACCALLUM
No, no! I'm fine here. I want to get used to the Court, you see. I'm forty miles from home, you understand, and I just feel like a fish out of water.

#### COURT OFFICER
Ach, don't be exciting yourself now.

#### MACCALLUM
(*Looking at a yellow paper in his hand.*) What a lot of "saids" and "aforesaids" they put into a summons!

#### COURT OFFICER
Well, that's the law, you see. When a lawyer's making a speech he feels fine if he says "aforesaid" every now and again.

#### MACCALLUM
Do you tell me now? I never thought of that! (HE *reads.*) "The sheep aforesaid" — yes, yes — you'd think it was a very special sheep, if you said it that way. I wonder now if I could be trying that myself when I'm giving my evidence. "Rory MacColl aforesaid." That's fine!

#### COURT OFFICER
Ach, now, don't you be trying any of that nonsense!

#### MACCALLUM

Well, I'll just be going over in my own mind what I'll be saying to the Sheriff; and then I'll feel more at home when he comes in, you understand. This will be the witness-box?

*(He crosses to the witness-stand.*

#### COURT OFFICER

It is that.

#### MACCALLUM

There would be no harm in my standing in it for a wee minute, just to accustom myself to the way I would be feeling when my turn comes?

#### COURT OFFICER

No harm at all, Mr. MacCallum! Go you in and welcome!

#### MACCALLUM

Och, you're very kind—very kind—indeed, yes. *(He goes to the witness-stand, and holds up his right hand, mumbling over the words of the oath to himself, then smiles, bows and steps down.)* Yes, yes, I'll be doing fine. All the same I'd feel easier if my lawyer was with me this day.

#### COURT OFFICER

And have you no lawyer then for this case?

#### MACCALLUM

Well, I was to have had Mr. Thomson from the Oban— the young one—the good one; but the ten o'clock steamer could not take the pier this morning because of the high wind; and the poor man will have been carried on to Mallaig most likely. It's a good thing I came myself by last night's steamer.

#### COURT OFFICER

It's a peety for Mr. Thomson being taken so far out of his way.

#### MACCALLUM

Och, well, it's a lawyer's fee saved. And I'll do as well as any lawyer when it comes to the bit.

#### COURT OFFICER

All the same I like to see a man with his lawyer when a Court is held.

#### MACCALLUM

But, man, man! What need of a lawyer when I saw Rory kill the sheep with my own eyes? A fine sheep it was, too—as fine a gimmer as ever you saw, Mr. MacConnachie.

**COURT OFFICER**

So I was hearing; but you're forty miles away as you say, and we didna hear much of the business at this end of the country.

*(The door opens, and* **RORY MACCOLL** *comes in. He is a Highland shepherd, aged sixty, and carries a cromag, or long crook of hazel. His bearded face is old and weathered, as is also his suit of rough homespun. His eyes are sharp and twinkling. At sight of him* **MACCALLUM** *turns away in disgust.)*

**RORY**

A fine day, Mr. MacCallum.

*(MacCallum does not reply.* **RORY** *looks up and round the Court-house inquiringly. The* **COURT OFFICER** *goes towards him.)*

**COURT OFFICER**

Good day! Are you in this case?

**RORY**

I am that. It's a great stack of stones, this Courthouse. What time will you be wanting me?

*(He hands some yellow papers to the* **COURT OFFICER**.

**COURT OFFICER**

*(Reading them.)* Ach! it's you, is it? — Rory MacColl. Eleven o'clock. You'll be having half an hour to wait.

**RORY**

Half an hour! Is there an Inns in this place.

**COURT OFFICER**

There is that. But if I were you, I'd not go near the Inns till your case is over. There's a fire in the waiting-room out there.

**RORY**

But they'll have a fire in the Inns, too?

**COURT OFFICER**

I'm thinking the waiting-room fire will be safer for the like of you, Rory.

**RORY**

*(Grinning, as he goes out easily.)* Well, I could be taking a look at both of them, surely.

**MACCALLUM**

*(Fuming.)* Did you hear that? The cheek of him! Killing my sheep, and then wishing me a good day, as cool as you like!

**COURT OFFICER**

So that's the man, is it? What way did you not have the police take him up on a criminal charge?

#### MACCALLUM

'Deed and I don't know why the police would not do that same, when I asked them. They just said there was too much sheep's-head broth in it, and advised me to claim for damages.

#### COURT OFFICER

Only a small debt case, is it? Well, well!

#### MACCALLUM

Aye, just that. But wait you, and see if it will not turn out a perjury case, before we're done with it. Wait till you hear Rory swearing away his soul this day! You never heard his like for the great flow of language. English or Gaelic, it's all the same to Rory—there's no stopping the lying tongue of him!

#### COURT OFFICER

As bad as that!

#### MACCALLUM

Aye, as bad as that! Wait you! For if this place is not struck by lightning as soon as Rory opens his dirty mouth, my name is not Duncan MacCallum.

#### COURT OFFICER

Ach, if it's lies brings down the lightning, this place would have been rock and lime long ago.

#### MACCALLUM

Well, well! And is that the way of it?
(MR. MACINTOSH, *a lawyer from Oban, enters, carrying a black gown on his arm. He is a man of fifty, clean-shaven, and bald-headed. He has narrow, quizzing eyes.*

#### COURT OFFICER

Good day, Mr. MacIntosh.

#### MACINTOSH

Oh, good day, Mr. MacConnachie. Look here, this isn't the gown I left here a week ago.

#### COURT OFFICER

I'm sorry, Mr. MacIntosh. Some of the other lawyers must have taken yours last Tuesday. Just you be doing with that one for the present.

#### MACINTOSH

It's a confounded nuisance, you know.
(*He turns to go out.*

#### MACCALLUM

*(Coming forward.)* Good day to you, sir!

#### MACINTOSH

Oh, good day! I'm afraid I haven't the pleasure of knowing you.

#### COURT OFFICER

This is the pursuer, sir—Mr. MacCallum of Ardnish.

#### MACCALLUM

Yes, yes. Now isn't it strange that you'll not remember me? You got some Harris tweed out of my shop at Ardnish, a year ago last August.

#### MACINTOSH

Ardnish? I was never in Ardnish all my life, I'm sorry to say. But a fine place, I hear.

#### MACCALLUM

Och, yes, but you *were* in Ardnish. Yes, yes—a year ago last August. And I mistook you for a Mr. MacFarlane, a great salmon-fisher that was staying at Ardnish Hotel.

#### MACINTOSH

Well, I'm no salmon-fisher, Mr. MacCallum. And I was never in Ardnish at any time. You're mistaken.

#### MACCALLUM

Am I saying you are a salmon-fisher? ... All I'm saying is that there were many strangers about that day, and you were one of them. And the name you had then was not MacIntosh, but MacFarlane.

#### MACINTOSH

Sir, do you doubt my word? I tell you again I was never in Ardnish in all my life!

#### MACCALLUM

Och, yes, but you were. A year ago last August. And off you went just in time to catch the steamer. And that tweed was never paid for. And me not seeing you from that day to this.

#### MACINTOSH

Is this a joke, sir?

#### MACCALLUM

No joke about it. Never a penny did I get from you.

#### MACINTOSH

I tell you, sir, it must have been somebody else.

#### MACCALLUM

And I tell you I never forget a face or a voice. And what I say to you is: Pay me for the tweed you stole away from me a year ago last August.

#### MACINTOSH

Stole? — stole? You hear what this man says, MacConnachie? (*He takes out paper and pencil, and makes a note hurriedly.*) He accuses me of theft, and I take you as a witness.

#### COURT OFFICER

Ach, no, no! I've enough to do with putting other people into the witness-box, let alone myself! For goodness' sake, be settling it among yourselves!

#### MACINTOSH

But this is too serious a matter to pass over, Mr. MacConnachie. Excuse me a moment. (**HE** *goes to the door at back, and calls.*) Mr. MacColl! (**RORY** *enters.*) This isn't your case yet, Mr. MacColl. But something almost as important. (**MACCALLUM** *moves away, but* **MACINTOSH** *puts a hand on his arm.*) Just a moment, sir. Will you now have the kindness to repeat before this good man the words you have just used about myself?

#### MACCALLUM

Good man? And who are you calling a good man? (*Then to* **RORY**.) Well, you may be a good man, as Neil of the Mountain said to the cat, but you haven't the face of one.

#### RORY

And who are you to be talking? You're nothing but a whistle and a noise, when all's said and done. Man, man! you'd make a stirk laugh.

#### MACINTOSH

Never mind, Mr. MacColl. Just let him repeat what he said a moment ago in the presence of Mr. MacConnachie here.

#### MACCALLUM .

'Deed, and I'll do nothing so foolish. But I'll be seeing my lawyer to-morrow, about you and my Harris tweed.

#### MACINTOSH

What Harris tweed?

#### MACCALLUM

The Harris tweed you stole from me a year ago last August.

#### MACINTOSH

Ah! I thought that would fetch you. You heard, Rory? He said "stole."

#### RORY

He did that.

#### MACCALLUM

Och, I'll be staying here no longer with such a pair of thieves.

**RORY**

Well, it's a poor pair that's no match for one.

*(MacCallum flounces out, shouting.*

**MACCALLUM**

I said thieves and I'll stick to it, look you!

**MACINTOSH**

You observe, Rory? He said "thieves". You heard, MacConnachie.
Please take a note, both of you.

*(He scribbles industriously himself.*

**COURT OFFICER**

Ach, I'm not taking any notes. I've my own work to attend to.

*(He goes out angrily.*

**MACINTOSH**

*(Still scribbling.)* All right. Please take a note, Rory, that Mr.
MacConnachie refuses to take a note.

**RORY**

Och, no need for notes, for I'll be minding all he said. And I'm no
scholar with the pen, anyway.

**MACINTOSH**

*(Shutting his notebook with a snap, angrily.)* The idea! Why, I never was in
Ardnish in all my life! Called me a thief, did he? Well, he'll find it's not
one penny will settle this little business!

**RORY**

Yes, yes! But about my own case, now? You were saying you would be
giving me the good advice before the Court started.

**MACINTOSH**

It's awkward doing that here. Somebody might come in. And we've lost
time, too, with that fool. *(HE makes for the door, but turns.)* No, we can't
go into the witness-room now. Tell you what. Put your foot against that
door. *(RORY does so.)* Thank you. And now I'll give you a few hints. *(HE
paces up and down, cogitating.)* The old ruffian! Called me a thief! Well,
we'll see. Tuts! Him and his Harris tweed!

**RORY**

I wish you'd leave that Harris tweed alone, and tell me what to say
about the sheep I killed.

**MACINTOSH**

Aha! So you did kill it? Last Tuesday you told me that you didn't kill it!

**RORY**

Yes, yes; I told you that.

**MACINTOSH**

Well, will you go into that box to-day and swear on oath that you did not kill it?

**RORY**

Look you! Some of them poor sheep are that bad with the braxy they're far better killed.

**MACINTOSH**

I know all that. But will you take your oath that you did not kill MacCallum's sheep?

**RORY**

Och, take an oath, is it?

**MACINTOSH**

Yes.

**RORY**

No, no! I have my religion; and I'll take no oath.

**MACINTOSH**

You say you did not kill this sheep?

**RORY**

(Hesitatingly.) No.

**MACINTOSH**

Then why not swear as before Almighty God that you didn't?

**RORY**

Och, no! I have my religion, you'll understand. I'm not liking that oath at all, at all.

**MACINTOSH**

Well, what are you going to tell the sheriff?

**RORY**

I'll tell him MacCallum didn't see me kill the sheep.

**MACINTOSH**

But MacCallum will swear that he did see you.

**RORY**

Och, no, it was too dark that night. He couldna see me.

**MACINTOSH**

Man alive! You'll lose your case, if you say that! Look here, Rory! Unless you promise to take the oath, and say you didn't kill that sheep, I'll fling up your case.

**RORY**

Now, now, Mr. MacIntosh, be you a good man! Don't you be angry with poor Rory. See you this! *(He turns out a dirty purse.)* Look at the good pound notes I have for paying you—that is, if I'll win the case.

**MACINTOSH**

My good fellow, you must pay me, I'm afraid, whether you win or lose.

**RORY**

Och, is it pay you, if I lose? No, no!

**MACINTOSH**

Look here, you old humbug! I've had enough of this. You must promise me here and now to settle up as soon as the case is finished. Otherwise, I'm off home with the one o'clock steamer.

**RORY**

Och, very well! The man that divides the pudding will have the thick end to himself, I can see! But I'll promise, if there are to be no oaths.

**MACINTOSH**

You are a stubborn old mule. Why! the Sheriff won't hear you, unless you take the oath.

**RORY**

I could be having a sore throat, look you, and no can speak.

**MACINTOSH**

Good! But no—that won't do. He'd ask you to nod your head very likely as he repeated the oath to you. Tell you what, though! Say something silly every time he addresses you, or when anyone speaks to you at all. Understand?

**RORY**

*(Parrot fashion.)* "Something silly."

**MACINTOSH**

You are an ass! Aha! I've got it. You're not an ass, Rory, you're a sheep!

**RORY**

Is it me—a sheep?

**MACINTOSH**

Yes, a sheep. And every time you're spoken to by way of question you must answer like a sheep. Like this— *Meh!* Understand?

**RORY**

*Meh!*

**MACINTOSH**

Splendid. The Sheriff will think you're off your head, and ask you to stand down. Besides, since MacCallum has no lawyer with him he's sure to mix his case all up. We're in luck, old son, we're in luck! Ha-ha!

**RORY**

Aye, laugh away! But it may be no laughing for me, if the Sheriff gets cross. Man, man! if I had a boil, and you squeezing it, you'd still be laughing.

**MACINTOSH**

Sorry, Rory! No offence! But, tell me, who is MacCallum's agent? It's quite true, isn't it, that he was carried past the pier in the ten o'clock steamer?

**RORY**

Yes, it's true enough. It was Mr. Thomson from the Oban.

**MACINTOSH**

Well, he can't get back to-day, anyway. Good thing I took the eight o'clock boat, or where would you have been, eh?

**RORY**

*Meh!*

**MACINTOSH**

Splendid! You'll look as daft as Lachie Gorra! And MacCallum will be no better when I've finished cross-examining him, let me tell you. Besides, the Sheriff will be in a hurry. He always expects a round of golf before lunch on a Tuesday, if I know his little ways. You watch him scuttling off, as soon's we're through. Fine! Fine! (**HE** *rubs his hands. There is a sound of voices outside the door at right.*) Hush! They're coming! Quick! Take your foot away from that door now.

    (**THEY** *both come forward into the body of the Courthouse.*

**COURT OFFICER**

(*Entering with* **MACCALLUM**.) Will you please sit here, Mr. MacCallum? (*He indicates table.*)

**MACCALLUM**

Thank you, Mr. MacConnachie.
    (*He sits down at table, and, drawing out his notes, cons them carefully.*
  **MACINTOSH** *takes a seat at the opposite end of the table, and refers to his*
                       *papers also.*

**COURT OFFICER**

(To **RORY**.) You'll sit here, Rory. (*He indicates the front bench, facing the Sheriff's desk.*)

RORY

*Meh!*

COURT OFFICER

What did you say?

RORY

*Meh!*

(MACCALLUM *looks up in astonishment. Some of the* CROFTERS *and* TOWNSFOLK *who have entered titter, as they take their seats in the back benches. The* COURT OFFICER *goes out, and ushers in the* SHERIFF, *bewigged and gowned.*

COURT OFFICER

Court!

(*All stand, and after the* SHERIFF *has taken his seat sit again. The* COURT OFFICER *whispers to the* SHERIFF, *pointing to* MACCALLUM. *The Sheriff puts his hand to his ear, and says: "Eh?" The* COURT OFFICER *whispers more loudly. It is evident that his lordship is slightly deaf: and from the way he peers at his papers it is also clear that he doesn't see very well. Throughout the trial his deafness and defective vision are clearly indicated by his various gestures. At times he does not make out who is addressing whom.*

SHERIFF

Ah, most unfortunate! I'm sorry, Mr. MacCallum, to hear that your solicitor has been carried past the pier, because of the storm this morning. That is so, isn't it?

MACCALLUM

Yes, my lord.

SHERIFF

Then I suppose you will put forward your own case?

MACCALLUM

If you please, my lord.

SHERIFF

Very well. Go on.

(MACCALLUM *nods to the* COURT OFFICER, *who goes out by door at back.*

COURT OFFICER

*(In a loud voice.)* Mrs. MacLean!

(MRS. MACLEAN, *a stout Highland crofter-woman, with a shock of red hair, appears. She is flustered, and has an aggressive air, as She is ushered into the witness-box.*

SHERIFF

You are Mrs. MacLean, Ardnish?

**MRS. MACLEAN**

Yes, my lord.

**SHERIFF**

(*Holding up right hand.*) "I swear by Almighty God."

**MRS. MACLEAN**

(*Holding up right hand.*) "I swear by Almighty God."

**SHERIFF**

"As I shall answer to God."

**MRS. MACLEAN**

"As I shall answer to God."

**SHERIFF**

"At the great day of judgment."

**MRS. MACLEAN**

" At the great day of judgment."

**SHERIFF**

"That I will tell the truth."

**MRS. MACLEAN**

"That I will tell the truth."

**SHERIFF**

"The whole truth."

**MRS. MACLEAN**

"The whole truth."

**SHERIFF**

"And nothing but the truth."

**MRS. MACLEAN**

"And nothing but the truth."

**MACCALLUM**

(*Rising and turning over his papers excitedly.*) Mrs. MacLean, was you very fond of sheep's-head broth?'

**MRS. MACLEAN**

I was that.

**SHERIFF**

Louder, please. I can't hear.

**MRS. MACLEAN**

I—was—that.

**SHERIFF**

Thank you.

**MACCALLUM**

Was it known to the defender, the aforesaid Rory MacColl, that you was very fond of sheep's-head broth?

**MRS. MACLEAN**

It was that.

**MACCALLUM**

Did he ask yourself and Widow MacIver to a meal of sheep's-head broth on the day of the 28th March last?

**MRS. MACLEAN**

Was that a Thursday?

**MACCALLUM**

It was that.

**SHERIFF**

A little louder, please. What did you say, Mr. MacCallum.

**MACCALLUM**

I said, " It was that," O lord—I mean, my lord.

**SHERIFF**

Thank you! Go on, Mrs. MacLean. Tell us if that Thursday was the 28th of March.

**MRS. MACLEAN**

Och, I'll no' can mind. But it was the day after Rory killed the sheep.

**SHERIFF**

Stop!—stop!—stop! You really must not say a thing like that. It has not yet been proved that anybody killed a sheep. Answer the question—no more. You mean that it was on the day after Mr. MacCallum's sheep was said to be killed?

**MRS. MACLEAN**

Said to be killed? It was killed. How else could we have the sheep's-head broth?

**SHERIFF**

But you must not say that. Just answer my question.

**MRS. MACLEAN**

And where could Rory have got a sheep's-head but from a sheep?

**SHERIFF.**

Ahem! I am afraid, Mr. MacCallum, I am trespassing on your field, but with your permission, I'll interrogate this witness myself.

(MACCALLUM *bows and sits down.*

**MACCALLUM**

Certainly, O lord.

**SHERIFF**

Now, Mrs. MacLean! You had a meal of sheep's-head broth with Rory MacColl on Thursday, the 28th day of March last? Is that so?

**MRS. MACLEAN**

It was a Thursday, anyway.

**SHERIFF**

But is there nothing you can remember which happened about that time that will help you to the exact date?

**MRS. MACLEAN**

Well, I saw Rory having the sheep's-head singed at the smiddy on the morning of the day we had the sheep's-head broth.

**SHERIFF**

Well, what morning was that?

**MRS. MACLEAN**

The morning after the night that Rory killed the sheep.

**SHERIFF**

(*More in sorrow than in anger.*) That will do, Mrs. MacLean. Any questions, Mr. MacIntosh?

**MACINTOSH**

No, my lord.

**SHERIFF**

Stand down, Mrs. MacLean.

(*The* COURT OFFICER *leads the bewildered* MRS. MACLEAN *out of the room.* MACCALLUM *leaves the table and enters the witness-box. He takes the oath in the same way as the former witness.*

**SHERIFF**

Well, tell us your story, Mr. MacCallum.

**MACCALLUM**

My lord, having lost of late half a score of sheep, without having had from the aforesaid Rory MacColl a satisfactory account of their decease—

**SHERIFF**

Did you say "disease"?

**MACCALLUM**

Any way you like it, my lord. They were dead, anyway, my lord—or as good as dead, for I never saw them after the first dipping.

**SHERIFF**

Yes, yes. Go on, please. Time is short, Mr. MacCallum. Never mind about the dipping.

**MACCALLUM**

I decided therefore to watch said defender, having suspected the deceased Rory—the aforesaid Rory—of having caused decease of sheep aforesaid.

(**MACINTOSH** *laughs audibly behind his hand, hanging his head.* **MACCALLUM** *hears him, and says angrily*): Aye, laugh away, MacIntosh! But I'm not forgetting that Harris tweed.

**SHERIFF**

(*Not perceiving the cause of the interruption.*) What's this? We don't want anything irrelevant. Please let us keep to our sheep.

**MACCALLUM**

Yes, my lord. And a fine sheep it was—as fine a gimmer as ever you saw. I watched Rory through a hole in the wall of the fank on the night of the 27th March last, and saw him kill the sheep—the said 27th of March being the night before the beforesaid sheep's-head broth was made by Rory aforesaid. (**MACINTOSH** *laughs again involuntarily.*) Aye, laugh away, Mr. MacIntosh, but I'll be even with you yet!

**SHERIFF**

What's that? Whatever are you talking about, sir?

**MACCALLUM**

I'm talking about the good Harris tweed that was stole from me, and never paid for, O lord!

**SHERIFF**

I really can't follow you, Mr. MacCallum. Let us come back to our sheep, if you please.

**MACCALLUM**

Very good, my lord. I saw Rory aforesaid cut off the head of my good gimmer before my very eyes, meaning said head, no doubt, for the sheep's-head broth to be made on the 28th March aforesaid. (**MACINTOSH** *laughs again.*) Yes, you may laugh! But all the same I'll make you pay for the ten yards of tweed you took away in your trap.

**SHERIFF**

Ten yards in a trap? Whatever are you saying now, Mr. MacCallum?
Who ever heard of ten yards of a sheep?

**MACCALLUM**

No, my lord. Ten yards of good Harris tweed. Crotal colour it was. And
it never paid for, since a year ago last August.

**SHERIFF**

I really don't follow you. Do, please, let us get back to our sheep.
I really wish you had a legal representative here, Mr. MacCallum.
Continue.

**MACCALLUM**

I saw him kill the sheep by cutting its throat first of all, my lord. And
then, thinking maybe of the aforesaid sheep's-head broth, he cut off
the sheep's-head to make the broth aforesaid. (**MACINTOSH** *chuckles once
more.*) Look at him laughing. But you did not laugh when you got into
your trap and drove off with the tweed you never paid for?

**SHERIFF**

Do I understand you to say that the defender caught the sheep in a
trap? Was it a variety of sheep known as a Harris sheep? I thought that
breed was extinct.

**MACCALLUM**

My lord, it wasn't the sheep that was in the trap. It was the tweed —
good Harris tweed, and crotal at that.

**SHERIFF**

Ah! You mean that the wool lost by the disappearance of the sheep was
equivalent to so much good Harris tweed? Is that it? If that is so, never
mind about the tweed just now. We are not concerned with the possible
products of the sheep.

**MACCALLUM**

Well, if your lordship will allow me to say so, I'm really more
concerned about the tweed than the sheep.

**SHERIFF**

Yes, yes, I know. But the sheep comes first, then the wool, then the
spinning and the dyeing, then the weaving of the tweed. I know all
that. But the sheep comes before the tweed, doesn't it?

**MACCALLUM**

Well, in this case it didn't, my lord. The tweed was stolen long before
the sheep was killed. It was a year ago last August.

**SHERIFF**

Ahem! I am afraid I must ask you to discontinue, Mr. MacCallum. Time is short; and I can't follow you into all these irrelevancies ... Now, Mr. Macintosh.

**MACINTOSH**

Mr. MacCallum, you say you saw the defender kill the sheep on the night of the 27th March last?

**MACCALLUM**

I did that.

**MACINTOSH**

At what o'clock did you see this?

**MACCALLUM**

About nine o'clock.

**MACINTOSH**

Was there a moon that night?

**MACCALLUM**

No.

**MACINTOSH**

Had defender a light in the fank?

**MACCALLUM**

No.

**MACINTOSH**

What kind of knife had he?

**MACCALLUM**

I did not see the knife.

**MACINTOSH**

You did not see the knife? Why?

**MACCALLUM**

It was too dark.

**MACINTOSH**

So that you could not see the knife; and yet you saw him kill the sheep?

**MACCALLUM**

I heard him swearing at the sheep, and saying he'd soon kill it. And then I heard the poor beast struggling and groaning, and then it stopped all at once.

**MACINTOSH**

Ah! So you did not really *see* him kill the sheep? You heard him kill the sheep?

**MACCALLUM**

Yes. I heard him kill the sheep.

**MACINTOSH**

You heard some sounds, and you thought those sounds came from a sheep in process of being killed?

**MACCALLUM**

I heard him kill the sheep.

**MACINTOSH**

I understand. You admit, then, that you did not see him kill the sheep.

**MACCALLUM**

I heard him kill the sheep.

**MACINTOSH**

Very well. Now, Mr. MacCallum, attend to me! Will you please tell his lordship if it is not the case that a sheep struggles and groans if some one gives it a dose of medicine?

**MACCALLUM**

It might well do that.

**MACINTOSH**

So that the struggling and groaning you heard might not have been the sounds of a sheep in process of being killed.

**MACCALLUM**

I heard him kill the sheep.

**MACINTOSH**

Very well. Now, will you please explain to his lordship what you mean when you say that you saw the defendant with a sheep of the species called Harris, and measuring ten yards; the said sheep being caught in a trap?

**MACCALLUM**

Never you mind what I mean, Mr. MacIntosh, or Mr. MacFarlane or whatever your name is! ... But I say you stole a roll of Harris tweed from me in Ardnish, a year ago last August; and it's never paid for yet!

**MACINTOSH**

*(Sitting down.)* Thank you.

**SHERIFF**

That will do, Mr. MacCallum. Stand down.

(**MACCALLUM**, *fuming, is led back to his seat at the table by the* **COURT OFFICER**. **RORY** *is then taken to the witness-box, at a sign from* **MACINTOSH**.

**COURT OFFICER**

You're next, Rory.

**MACINTOSH**

His name is Rory MacColl, my lord—the defender, aged sixty-two. He hasn't much English.

**SHERIFF**

*(Writing.)* Very good. *(Then, holding up his right hand.)* "I swear by Almighty God." *(RORY is silent.)* Repeat after me. " I swear"—He has some English, hasn't he, Mr. MacIntosh?

**MACINTOSH**

Oh, yes, my lord.

**SHERIFF**

Can you hear me?

**RORY**

*Meh!*

**SHERIFF**

What do you say?

**RORY**

*Meh!*

**SHERIFF**

I beg pardon. Again.

**RORY**

*Meh!*

**SHERIFF**

Is this man *compos mentis*, Mr. MacIntosh?

**MACINTOSH**

He has certainly been very queer of late, my lord. Indeed, ever since this dreadful charge has been levelled against him he has been odd in his manner. He has always been of a gentle, trustful nature. And, now that he finds the harsh realities of the world quite other than he had dreamt them to be, it may quite well have fallen out that his mind has become unhinged.

**SHERIFF**

My dear sir, if there are many more witnesses in this case like this man and his two predecessors, my own mind will certainly become unhinged. See what you can make of him; and then I'll sum up the case.

**MACINTOSH**

Thank you, my lord. Now attend to me, Mr. MacColl. Did you ever at any time or under any circumstances kill a sheep belonging to Mr. MacCallum?

**RORY**

*Meh!*

**MACINTOSH**

Answer me properly, please. Where did you get the sheep's head, of which you made a broth?

**RORY**

*Meh!*

**MACINTOSH**

Can't you understand what I say?

**RORY**

*Meh!*

**MACINTOSH**

*(To the SHERIFF, who is listening intently, with his hand at his ear.)* I am afraid it's no use, my lord. The poor man's head has been turned by this ordeal.

**SHERIFF**

*(Drily.)* Yes. Just so. I am afraid, Mr. MacIntosh, you also are of a gentle, trustful disposition. This man may be as you say, yet other explanations are possible. But time is short; and we need not go into that. The defender is evidently — evidently, I say, unable to give us any help. The pursuer's case rests on that of Mrs. MacLean and himself. The fact that Mrs. MacLean supped off sheep's-head broth along with the defender on a date of great uncertainty is no doubt of interest, but it is irrelevant. And the pursuer's evidence is also unsatisfactory. He did not see defender kill the sheep. He only heard some sounds, which he interpreted as those emitted by a sheep in its death-agony. I am not an authority on the sounds emitted by sheep, although after listening to Mr. MacColl's performance in the witness-box, I feel as if, with a little further study, I might qualify as such. But one does not require to be such an authority to see that Mr. MacCallum may have misinterpreted the sounds he heard. I express my regret that Mr. MacCallum's solicitor was not here to help him with his case. Judgment for the defender, with expenses.

*(HE rises to go, and all stand as HE retires. The COURT OFFICER follows; and the people crowd round RORY, congratulating him. RORY only grins and returns numerous handshakes without uttering a word. MACCALLUM strides over to MACINTOSH.*

**MACCALLUM**

You'll hear more about that tweed before very long, my hero.

*(But* **MACINTOSH** *only sniggers happily as* **HE** *makes out an account for* **RORY***; and* **MACCALLUM** *goes off, furious.* **MACINTOSH** *rises with his bill, and interrupts the rejoicings over* **RORY***'s victory.*

**MACINTOSH**

Here you are, Rory. It should be five guineas, but we'll say five pounds. *(He hands* **RORY** *the bill.)*

**RORY**

*(Regarding the bill and then* **MACINTOSH***'s extended hand.)*
Meh!

**MACINTOSH**

Come on, you old rascal! Five pounds.

**RORY**

*Meh-h-h!*

# CURTAIN

# The Happy War

Persons

| | |
|---|---|
| The MÉDECIN-CHEF | *Dr. Bowlby of the Anglo-French Unit (Croix Rouge Française) at Chateau d'Aulnoy.* |
| DR. PEARSON | *His Assistant.* |
| KOECHLIN | *Wounded French soldier under their care, now convalescent.* |
| The Boches | *Two escaped prisoners from the cages at Courbon.* |

THE TIME is September, 1917.
THE PLACE is the Haute Marne, France.

*Scene.* — *A room in a deserted monastery in the Haute Marne, France, on a late afternoon in September, 1917. It is a bare chamber with white-washed walls and brown timber beams; the plaster broken and rain-stained in places. There is a large door in the back wall, fully open; and through it is seen a sunlit forest-glade. On either side of the door is a high lanceolate window, dusty and broken-paned. There are also doors, somewhat tiny, in the walls to left and right; the right door being well forward, the left well back. All the doors have old iron scroll-work near their locks and bossed nail-heads studding their planching.*

*There is a large open fire-place, with smouldering charcoal, well forward in the wall on left. Near the back, and close to the same wall, is a rudely fashioned bed of timber with the bark still adherent. A similar bed stands close to the right wall. On both beds the coverings are in disarray. A plain kitchen table and several boxes serviceable for seats are ranged before the fire-place. A khaki overcoat hangs on the back wall between the right window and the main door.*

*Through the door at the rear the* MÉDECIN-CHEF *slouches in. He is a man of fifty-three, grey-haired and clean-shaven, with a figure tending to corpulency; his countenance somewhat blowsy. His tunic is unbuttoned, his cap tilted backwards, and he is generally untidy. He carries a fishing-rod and a string of trout; a khaki knapsack is slung over his shoulder; protruding from it is the handle of a small frying-pan. His uniform is the ordinary khaki; but the facings on it are the blue facings of the Croix Rouge Française (Comité Britannique).*

*He lays his fishing-rod and fish on the table, and un-slinging his knapsack, unpacks the frying-pan and sets it by the fire. He is humming the French marching tune "Madelon" all the while; and going out by door on right, returns with a loaf of French pattern and a mug.*

#### DISTANT VOICE

*(Heard through open door.)* Hilly hoy!

*(The* MÉDICIN-CHEF *goes to door and looks vaguely round, shading his eyes, then waves his hand, calling:*

#### MÉDECIN-CHEF

Hullo—hullo!

*(After an interval of some seconds* DR. PEARSON *enters, a man of thirty, attired in the same uniform as the* MÉDECIN-CHEF. PEARSON, *however, is neat and dapper, as befits his slight build. He has a business-like air.*

#### PEARSON

Well, you're the last man I expected to see, sir. Lost my way in those confounded woods!

#### MÉDECIN-CHEF

They are a bit dense, aren't they?

#### PEARSON

Yes—but—! Well—really—!—Why, every one in hospital thinks you're two hundred miles away, sir.

MÉDECIN-CHEF

Officially I am, dear boy. And I've no doubt the trout in the Aujon wish I were! *(Lifts fishing-rod gaily.)*

PEARSON

Queer! Only six miles from Hospital—and yet here you are in a perfect solitude—the heart of the forest, eh?

MÉDECIN-CHEF

Oh! I got fed up with operating. Nervy, you know—

PEARSON

Gets me that way too, at times.

MÉDECIN-CHEF

So I do the mighty hunter all by my lonesome.— Thoreau, and that sort of thing, you see.

PEARSON

Lucky for you, sir!

MÉDECIN-CHEF

Oh, chuck the "sir", PEARSON. Less red tape! I'm on holiday, y' know.

PEARSON

Very good, sir!

MÉDECIN-CHEF

Again? Naughty, naughty! But I must tell you about the fishing here. Got a whacker yesterday—three pounds if it was an ounce.—Like this—!
*(He indicates a huge fish with his hands apart.*

PEARSON

Golly, what a whale!

MÉDECIN-CHEF

Didn't exactly get him—but I hooked him, anyway. Made a great fight, and then went off with my best fly.

PEARSON

By gum!

MÉDECIN-CHEF

Four pounds if he was anything.

PEARSON

Makes my teeth water!

MÉDECIN-CHEF

*(Enthusing more and more.)* And there's a corker in a pool, not a kilometre from. here. Mean to get him some day soon.—Big as this—
*(He extends his hands farther still.*

**PEARSON**

*(Rallying him.)* Gad! Aren't you frightened with all those monsters about?

**MÉDECIN-CHEF**

*(Discovering he has overdone the fishing-story business.)* Oh! come off it, young 'un!

**PEARSON**

Really nobody here but yourself?

**MÉDECIN-CHEF**

Nary a soul! I'm my own cook and my own orderly. And except for wood-cutters now and then, this place is quite deserted. All I need is my rod, my frying-pan, some bread, and a letter from mother.

**PEARSON**

Letter from mother?

**MÉDECIN-CHEF**

Yes. *(Taking out an envelope and shaking it.)* Handy for pepper and salt. And I get milk and apples from a farm four kilometres off.

**PEARSON**

Sleep here?

**MÉDECIN-CHEF**

Yes. Beds left by wood-cutters last fall. — Jolly old place this! A bunch of monks have been around here in the old days. There's a fine fresco — a Crucifixion — in the salle through there. *(Pointing to the door on right.)*

**PEARSON**

*(Looking at beds.)* Two of 'em. Kind of them to have thought of me.

**MÉDECIN-CHEF**

No, you don't, sonny. You're going back to Hospital. And by the by, you haven't yet told me why you aren't there at the present moment.

**PEARSON**

Looking for strays, sir.

**MÉDECIN-CHEF**

Breakers of bounds? Again?

**PEARSON**

Yes. Old KOECHLIN's been out all night — the leg case.

**MÉDECIN-CHEF**

There were two KOECHLINS — both leg wounds. Is it the Marseilles chap?

No. The Alsace Johnny.

#### MÉDECIN-CHEF

Ugh! Women, I suppose?

#### PEARSON

No, sir. I fancy he's on the hunt after those escaped Boches—from the Courbon cages.

#### MÉDECIN-CHEF

Never heard of any escaped Boches. Must have been after I left yesterday.

#### PEARSON

So it was. Just after you'd gone we heard of it. A charcoal-burner saw them in the Chameroy forest. The gendarmerie all over the country are after them.

#### MÉDECIN-CHEF

Then why the devil doesn't KOECHLIN leave them to the gendarmerie?

#### PEARSON

Oh, sport, I suppose. He's fed-up—waiting on his leg healing. Anyway, he told old Renaud he'd like a pot at them, borrowed his field-glass and revolver, and vanished since noon yesterday.

#### MÉDECIN-CHEF

Oh, damn these mixed units! I'd rather be handling our own Tommies, PEARSON! Discipline's all to pigs and whistles with English people bossing Frenchies, like our push, you know.

(HE *goes to the fire and pokes it up.*

#### PEARSON

Don't I know!—And now we've several search-parties looking for KOECHLIN.—Old fool! I hope these Germans don't get him.
  (HE *is wandering round, looking at the iron-work on the doors, and fingering*
*it.*

#### MÉDECIN-CHEF

Oh! KOECHLIN will eat 'em up, game leg and all.— Whatever are you nosing round now?

#### PEARSON

This old iron-work. Real art this!

#### MÉDECIN-CHEF

(*Rising with the frying-pan in his hand.*) Yes, but you should see the fresco, laddie. Just come in here. This was the refectory, I fancy.

(*THEY go out by the door on the right, their footsteps sounding hollowly. They have just gone, when a* FIGURE *in the uniform of a German prisoner staggers in by the open door. He wears a German round cap, and a suit of dark fustian, with long trousers; over the knee of right leg is inserted a patch of bright blue cloth, eighteen inches by twelve, the mark of the Courbon prison-camp. He is emaciated; has dark hair and eyes, and a beard of a week's growth. A grey scarf, blood-stained, is knotted around his neck. He runs to the door on the right, listens, and then totters across to the door on the left, half-fainting, and enters the room to which it leads. He is gasping for breath as he disappears.*
THE MÉDECIN-CHEF *enters with* PEARSON *from the door on the right after a few seconds. He carries a bottle of wine and a cup.*)

PEARSON

Six pounds! And you got it with a fly?

MÉDECIN-CHEF

Well, not quite six. Maybe five, y' know.

PEARSON

And with a fly?

MÉDECIN-CHEF

Well—er—a grasshopper, in fact.

PEARSON

A grasshopper! Call yourself a sportsman?

MÉDECIN-CHEF

Well, you want to make sure, when you see a six-pounder.

PEARSON

Five, sir, I think you said!

MÉDECIN-CHEF

Well, say five and a half!—You see there was a grassy patch there; and I was lying—

PEARSON

Yes, sir, lying?

MÉDECIN-CHEF

DR. PEARSON!—I think it is time you returned to duty.

PEARSON

But you said something about less red tape!

MÉDECIN-CHEF

You young monkey! (*He grins.*)

All right, sir. I won't interrupt.

MÉDECIN-CHEF

Let me see. Where was I?

PEARSON

You were fishing *and* lying—

MÉDECIN-CHEF

*(Making a lunge at him.)* I'll be the death of you!

PEARSON

*(Skipping back and putting up his hands in a sparring attitude.)* No use, sir. Boxing's my forte. Yours is fishing.

MÉDECIN-CHEF

Coward! But tell me about the Hospital. Any "take-in" since I left?

PEARSON

One, last night. From Verdun. Twenty cases. Pretty so-so.—No bad wounds. Two amputations below the knee this morning.

MÉDECIN-CHEF

Beatson still punning, eh?

PEARSON

You bet: daily. This morning at breakfast he helped me to an omelette. I said, "Thanks, enough." Says he, "It is *un oeuf*".

MÉDECIN-CHEF

Eh?

PEARSON

See—*un oeuf*. French, y' know, for an egg.

MÉDECIN-CHEF

The beggar should be shot.—Well, and how about the nurses? Any picnics on?

PEARSON

The only one I've heard of is being organised for a fortnight hence.

MÉDECIN-CHEF

What's the occasion?

PEARSON

To celebrate your safe return from the dangers of Paris, sir.
        *(He keeps out of reach again, as the* MÉDECIN-CHEF *lunges at him.*

MÉDECIN-CHEF

You young dog! *(A groan is heard from the room on the left.)* What's that?

**PEARSON**

Some one in there. Got your gun handy, sir?

**MÉDECIN-CHEF**

*(Drawing revolver and going to room.)* We'll jolly soon see.
*(He pushes open the door and is followed by* **PEARSON**. *As* **HE** *makes to move into the room, he halts and says:*
Hillo, he's down—a Boche!—Let's take him out to the light.
*(They enter, reappear supporting the fainting German and carry him to the bed on the left, where they deposit him.*

**PEARSON**

By God!—he's got it bad. His forearm's smashed! Blood! Look at this!
*(He wipes his finger on the wounded man's tunic.)*

**MÉDECIN-CHEF**

Brandy!
*(He dashes off to the room on right, and reappears with a flask, which he applies to the man's lips. Then taking his coat off nail, he covers him.*
Keep him warm!
*(*PEARSON *takes off his coat also and flings it over the German.*

**PEARSON**

He's done for.

**MÉDECIN-CHEF**

Sure? Yes,—not a flutter. *(He touches an eyeball with his finger.)* Yes,—he's gone out! Poor devil! Must have lost a deal of blood from that arm. Let's put him back.
*(They carry him to the room on left and then return to the fire.*
Well, well!—Nothing but trouble!

**PEARSON**

I suppose I'd better ring up the authorities at Marac and report this.

**MÉDECIN-CHEF**

Oh, yes. But no hurry. They'll be fussing round here soon enough with their interrogatories and what not.

**PEARSON**

*(Starting.)* Sh—sh! *(He is looking through the open door.)* Here's the other Boche, I do believe!—See?— Crouching behind that bush to the left.— See his head?

**MÉDECIN-CHEF**

By Jove, you're right! He's on hands and knees!— Watch out! He may have us sighted!—There! He's rising!—Why, it's a French *kepi*!

KOECHLIN, I'll bet!—Yes! Isn't he the nippy one?— I believe he's tracked that poor beggar here! *(He draws his revolver, goes to door and calls.)* KOECHLIN!—*Arretez!*— *Approchez!*—*Vite!*

*(KOECHLIN comes to the doorway, limping; his hands above his head. He is in the horizon-blue undress uniform of the French hospital patient, but it is dust-stained and grimy. He is a man of forty. His sunburnt face is shaven; his eyes are dark and alert.*)

**MÉDECIN-CHEF**

Got you at last, you blighter!—All right. Drop your hands.

**PEARSON**

*(Noticing KOECHLIN shivering, He touches his cheek with his finger.)* By George, you're ill, KOECHLIN! You're in a fever! Sit down.

*(The MÉDECIN-CHEF hands him the flask of brandy, and he takes a pull at it.)*

**KOECHLIN**

*Mille remerciments, M. le Major.*

**MÉDECIN-CHEF**

Well, Koechlin,—nice business this, eh? You convalescents have the whole commune to wander through, and yet you must break bounds, eh?

**KOECHLIN**

Pardon! I will explain to M. le Major.

**MÉDECIN-CHEF**

As soon as I leave Hospital, you kick over the traces?

**KOECHLIN**

Pardon! I do not kick—

**MÉDECIN-CHEF**

No. But I will, if you chaps don't behave. There's too much French leave about you Frenchies!

**KOECHLIN**

But I will explain, M. le Major!

**MÉDECIN-CHEF**

*(Angrily.)* No, you won't. You'll tell me the whole bally truth, old cock. What took you off, eh?

**KOECHLIN**

I go to hunt the Boche who escape.

**PEARSON**

Didn't I tell you, sir?

And what business was that of yours? Aren't there gendarmerie enough?

**KOECHLIN**

*(In agony.) Oh! la-la!* The fresh and happy war!

**MÉDECIN-CHEF**

What the devil's he after now?

**PEARSON**

An epigram of the Crown Prince's.

**MÉDECIN-CHEF**

Fresh and happy war, eh? Must have been before Verdun, that.

**PEARSON**

You bet, sir.

**KOECHLIN**

*(Groaning.) Armand, mon pauvre Armand!*

**MÉDECIN-CHEF**

Armand? What's he gassing about now?

**KOECHLIN**

*Mon frère, monsieur.* —My brother, Armand! —Oh, it is difficult to tell. —We are of Alsace, Armand and myself... (**HE** *covers his face with his hands.)*

**MÉDECIN-CHEF**

*(Kindly.)* What's the trouble, old chap?

**KOECHLIN**

Ah! You will help, *monsieur*? Will you not? — We will find him, and you will make pardon for him.— Not so?

**MÉDECIN-CHEF**

Whatever is he getting at, PEARSON?

**PEARSON**

Not the faintest idea, sir.

**KOECHLIN**

Yes, *messieurs,* I will tell. —*Messieurs,* when, in July I see the war is to come—one month before it come, I hasten from Alsace to Switzerland, and then I go from Switzerland to France in time for the *mobilisation.* — But Armand, my brother, he is too late. —He is seized at the frontier and they force him to take arms for the Boches.

**MÉDECIN-CHEF**

Rotten luck!

**KOECHLIN**

And then last night, I hunt the escape Boches,—and *mon Dieu*! I find one in the wood here—and he is Armand!

**PEARSON**

My God! A brother?

**KOECHLIN**

*(Brokenly.)* But yes, *messieurs.*—*Oh, la-la!* The fresh and happy war!

**MÉDECIN-CHEF**

This is the limit, PEARSON!

**KOECHLIN**

Yes! Last night I see a man in the woods of Chameroy —He has the Boche *kepi.*—I call *'Halte-la!'*—He run.—I run.—I fire with the *pistolet.*—He fall.—I go to him.—But he is gone.—I lose him.—He has a grey scarf around the neck.

**MÉDECIN-CHEF**

Ah?

**KOECHLIN**

*(Unheeding the interruption.)* I search all night.—I search this morning.—All the woods—all the woods.—I think not at all of Armand.— I think only of a service *pour la France.*

**PEARSON**

Steady, old chap!

**KOECHLIN**

All night I search. The morning arrive.—And then one hour past, I come out on the Aubepierre road. I see something move in bushes—three hundred metres away—a man by the roadside. I take up *la jumelle. (He indicates the field-glasses hanging round his neck.)* I look at him. He is Boche. He has the grey scarf like the man I have wounded. And then he turn his face. *Et mon Dieu, monsieur!*—it is Armand, *mon frère!*
(HE *covers his face with his hands once more.*

**MÉDECIN-CHEF**

There, there! *(He claps him on shoulder.)* Rotten luck—rotten luck!

**KOECHLIN**

I call, *Armand!*—*Armand!*—*C'est moi!*—*Auguste! Ton frère!* But he run and run.—I throw away my *pistolet,*—and hold up my hands—so—and call and call.— But he is gone!—*mon Dieu!*—he is gone into the wood.—The wood is thick.—I lose him.—Then I see this place and find you.—And you will help, M. le Major,—you will help to find Armand.—Not so?—*Oh, la-la.* The happy war!

**MÉDECIN-CHEF**

A grey scarf, Koechlin?

**KOECHLIN**

But yes, colour of grey.

(The **MÉDECIN-CHEF** *exchanges glances with* **PEARSON**, *who nods,*
*unperceived by* **KOECHLIN**.

You will help, — M. le Major? — He is so wounded and so weak. — *Oh,*
*la-la!* — And truly, it is an affair that might have been — how you say? —
worse. — I might have killed him. — Also it is not the first time I have try.

**PEARSON**

Man alive! — Not the first time?

**KOECHLIN**

No, *messieurs*, not the first time. — At Mont Corneille on the Chemin des
Dames, — I have try. — His regiment and mine — we have opposed at two
hundred metres.

**MÉDECIN-CHEF**

Good Lord!

**KOECHLIN**

(*Sadly.*) But yes! — It was indeed the regiment of Armand. — We see the
*numero* on the uniforms of their dead. — It is the *numero* I have got in
letters from our friends in Switzerland. — *Quelle horreurs, messieurs!* — If I
do not fire, my comrades may suspect. — If I fire I may kill Armand. —
Figure to yourselves my desolation!

**PEARSON**

You have had trouble, and no mistake!

**KOECHLIN**

And now Armand is in this wood of the Calvaire. — Of that I am sure. —
And I can save him, if *messieurs* will only help.

**MÉDECIN-CHEF**

Poor old Koechlin. No, no! he isn't in the wood. Come here.
(**HE** *walks to the door of the room on the left, and signs to* **KOECHLIN** *to enter.*
**KOECHLIN** *looks within, utters a cry of agony, and crosses himself.*

**KOECHLIN**

*Pas mort? — Dites! — Pas mort? Ah, mon frère! — Armand! — Armand!*
(*He rushes into the room; then returns suddenly with the cap of the dead*
**BOCHE**, *which he tosses to the floor. He stamps upon it.*
*Attrapé, mon vieux, attrapé!* — You are to me! It is I who have killed! He is
**BOCHE**. He is not Armand!
(*He goes to the door of the room and shakes his fist.*

*Aha, mon vieux! — Attrapé! — Attrapé! — Attrapé! —* You are to me! — It is I who have killed!

PEARSON

*(Dragging him away.)* Here! Come off it! The poor beggar's dead!

KOECHLIN

*(Snapping finger and thumb at the still figure.) Attrapé!*

MÉDECIN-CHEF

Drop it, KOECHLIN. Cut off out o' this. Get back to Hospital and report! D'ye hear? Who knows but some of us may be like this poor devil before the day's over. Lump it!

KOECHLIN

But why you make trouble, M. le Major? He is Boche!

MÉDECIN-CHEF

Cut off, now!

KOECHLIN

Aha, you will not understand, you English! You live far away from the Boche. — You live not near them like us. — They are not men — these!

MÉDECIN-CHEF

Get off home, old chap. That's enough!

KOECHLIN

Ah! You have not seen! — You do not know what we French suffer from the Boche. — The village where there is no house — *dévastation.* The old men! — the women! — the little children! — *Oh, la-la!* I cannot tell.

PEARSON

*(Clapping him on the shoulder.)* All right, old boy. Glad it isn't your brother after all! And now get back to ba-ba, won't you? There's a good chap!

KOECHLIN

Yes, yes, I go.
> *(He turns to the open door. A shot suddenly rings out in the wood.*

MÉDECIN-CHEF

Hillo! More trouble!
> *(They all turn towards the main door. A wild* FIGURE *dashes in, dusty and unkempt. He is almost a replica of the first* BOCHE, *except that his suit is of a brown colour. He wears a grey scarf. He stares in amazement at the others, then wheels, as if to flee into the woods again. But* KOECHLIN *gives a wild cry of delight, rushes forward, and embraces him.*

**KOECHLIN**

Armand!

**NEWCOMER**

*Auguste! — Sauve-moi! — Les gendarmes!*
(*He points to the door, gasping.* **KOECHLIN** *runs to the door, looks out and*
*comes back to the* **MAJOR***, appealing.*

**KOECHLIN**

The gendarmes, M. le Major! You will save Armand— my brother? You
will explain!
(*Then turning to* **ARMAND***, He embraces him once more.*

**MÉDECIN-CHEF**

All right, all right, old chap. I'll explain.

**PEARSON**

(*Going to the door and looking out.*) Gendarmes, sure enough! Four of
them!

**MÉDECIN-CHEF**

Keep clear of that door, Pearson, for God's sake, or you'll stop a bullet!

**PEARSON**

Oh, all right! I've got my eyes peeled, sir.

**MÉDECIN-CHEF**

Keep away from that door, damn you! Do you hear? (*Shouting.*)
Pearson! Keep away from that door!
(*The* **HUNTED MAN***, who has been listening bewildered to a strange tongue*
*as he crouches by the wall, suddenly gets alarmed and makes a spring for the*
*door, as if he feared being trapped. A shot rings out, and he reels back, dead,*
*into* **KOECHLIN***'s arms.* **KOECHLIN***, dumb-foundered, supports him, and*
*looks round pathetically at the Englishmen as he lays him down, and kneels,*
*crossing himself. The* **MÉDECIN-CHEF** *covers his eyes with his hands.*

**PEARSON**

(*Kicking a box savagely, says bitterly.*) That's torn it! War!—my God!—
war!

# CURTAIN

# The Spanish Galleon

TIME: 1588
PLACE: Tobermory (Isle of Mull)
SCENE  John Smollett's Trading Quarters

Persons of the Play

| John Smollett | *Trader in the West Highlands* |
| Jonathan | *His Son* |
| Don Sebastian | *Son of the late Commander of the* |
| | *"San Juan Bautista",* |
| | *a Galleon of the Great Armada* |
| Ewan MacMorran | *A Mull Fisherman* |
| Barabel MacLean | *Daughter of a Mull Tacksman* |

*For the Play a Prelude has been composed by*
J. Seymour Halley

*First produced, by the Scottish National Players, in the Argyllshire
Gathering Hall, Oban, on 25th September 1922, under the direction of
A. P. Wilson, with the following cast:*

| *Ewan MacMorran* | R. B. Wharrie |
| *John Smollett* | A. P. Wilson |
| *Don Sebastian* | G. Paterson Whyte |
| *Jonathan* | Morland Graham |
| *Barabel MacLean* | Jean Taylor Smith |

SCENE: *A large apartment on the ground floor of* JOHN SMOLLETT'S *house, in an evening of late Autumn. Disposed around the walls are barrels of smoked salmon, bolls of meal, bags of salt, bundles of sheep-hides, spars, and fishing nets. To the left stands a desk, with a litter of papers and account-books, some tallow dips, and a ship's lantern. To the right is a small round table with drinking cups and a leathern bottle of wine. In the back wall is a large oaken door with stout wooden bar, and, left of this, in the same wall a small window, partly covered with coarse ragged sacking. A few steps go up to a chamber door in left wall; another door in the right wall gives access to house. Several chairs and stools are disposed about the room.*

JOHN SMOLLETT *and* EWAN MACMORRAN *sit drinking at the small table, casting furtive glances from time to time at the door on the left. Smollett is a sturdy man, about sixty, and of a slow heavy aspect, but masterly in temper, and with a certain portly dignity. He wears a brown doublet, loose Dutch trousers of the same colour, stockings of grey cloth, and buckled shoon. His wide hat lies on the table, and beside it a heavy knobbed walking-stick. MacMorran is a coarse man of the soil, shifty, cunning, quick to anger, but not incapable of a dog-like devotion. Age and rheumatism have somewhat enfeebled him; he wears a belted plaid, ragged and weather-stained.*

EWAN

Good wine, Mr Smollett.

SMOLLETT

Spanish.

EWAN

You tell me? From the big ship?

SMOLLETT

Aye. Frae the deid Captain's ain locker.

EWAN

I'll not be refusing another taste o't.

SMOLLETT

Canny now, Ewan. You'll need a clear heid for what's afore us the nicht. There you are. (*He fills a cup.*)

EWAN

Man, man, it's as mild as milk.

SMOLLETT

I wish this job was feenished. I'm in a sweat of anxiety. The crew's a turbulent lot, and mutinous forbye. It wouldna cost them a thocht to turn their guns on us—fire and sack the hale o' Tobermory.

**EWAN**

(*Laughing*) Aye: if Dol' MacLean is not first with his lunt among their pouther barrels.

**SMOLLETT**

Wheesht! Lodsake, if he should hear!
(**HE** *rises, and going towards the door on the left listens, then resumes his seat.*

**EWAN**

The young Spaniard? And will he still be sitting beside his father's corp?

**SMOLLETT**

Na, na. The body was smuggled oot yestreen under cloud o' nicht, and hidden in the chapel ruin upbye. He was to be secretly buried this morning afore cockcrow. If the crew suspected he was deid, they'd be neither to haud nor to bind.

**EWAN**

It's time them and their galleon was at the bottom of the Bay.

**SMOLLETT**

That's what Ashby writes me—the English Ambassador's man o' business, ye ken. But it's easier said than dune. Dol's a bold lad; but, if his fuse misses fire, they'll roast him alive, and we'll a' ha'e our throats slit. Yet it should be easier for him aince we get the hagbutmen ashore. What are ye wriggling and twisting at?

**EWAN**

I will be thinking it's not safe letting all those musketeers land here. It's not safe, look you, because it will be very dangerous.

**SMOLLETT**

But they're no' to bide here. Aren't they gaun ower to Loch Sunart on this splore o' MacLean's? Duart's aye in some bruilzie. He's ta'en his guidfaither prisoner; and now he's carryin' fire and sword against his ain mither!

**EWAN**

Yes, yes. A good gentlemanly Highland quarrel. A Sassenach will not understand.

**SMOLLETT**

I'm sure I dinna. The Loard send that baith sides get bluidy pates. The Spaniards want some fechtin'; and, faith! MacIan's men should gi'e them their fill o't. What fules the Spaniards were to seize Dol' MacLean for a hostage! And, dae ye ken! they've berthed him in a cabin beside the pouther magazine!

(*Shouts and crashes are heard at a distance.*

What hoyroyally's this? *(Rising and listening at the main door.)* Mair
Spaniards come ashore and brawling at the change-hoose.

#### EWAN

I tell you, it's not safe to let them off the ship.

#### SMOLLETT

Dinna worry me! Hoo can we stop them? I ken we're at the mercy
o' a crood o' redhanded Jesuitical cut-throats, itching to bring the
horrors o' the Inquisition back on us—the rack and the wheel and the
thumbscrew! I'd gledly blaw the hale clamjamfry o' them to the fower
winds of heaven!

> *(A loud knocking at the main door.)*

Losh, what's that?

#### VOICE

*(Outside.) Abra, abra!*

#### SMOLLETT

*(Going to the door)* Let me see *(Scratching his head)* . *Quien está ahí?*

#### VOICE

*Soy yo amigo.*

#### SMOLLETT

*(Going to the small stair and calling.)* Don Sebastian, Don Sebastian!
Here's anither Spanisher frae the ship.

(**DON SEBASTIAN** *enters by the door on the left. He is a young man of twenty-
eight, in the dress of a Spanish military officer. He has a dusky complexion,
black hair, and sharp, well-cut features. He carries himself proudly and has
something of the courtier's elegant, punctilious, almost flamboyant manner,
but at the moment his look is strained and anxious. He crosses to the main
door and opens it, giving a glimpse of the waters of the Bay, and a cloaked
figure seen against them. He goes out, shutting the door after him.*

#### EWAN

It's not happy he's looking, that one.

#### SMOLLETT

He has his ain troubles. The hale ship's seething wi' discontent. It's a
peety they ever won here. We'd be weel redd o' them.

#### EWAN

You can trust to Dol' and his fuse.

#### SMOLLETT

Wheesht, man, wheesht!

(**DON SEBASTIAN** *returns, and closes the main door. Worried-looking and with
bent head he goes towards his chamber.*

Weel, can you still keep up the appearance of the thing?

**SEBASTIAN**

Señor—you say?

**SMOLLETT**

I'm asking—do the crew suspect your faither's deid?

**SEBASTIAN**

No, *Madre de Dios!* not yet. It is those Castilians who are disaffected, and big Pedro. How will it end?

**SMOLLETT**

Ne'er fash your thoomb. The tussle wi' the MacDonalds'll tak' the pecher oot o' them. They'll be mair reasonable when they come back.

**SEBASTIAN**

You think?

**SMOLLETT**

I'm sure o't. That's why I advised you let them gang. But listen to that!
*(Shouts are heard as of drunken men singing in Gaelic "Gabhaidh sinn an rathad mor".*
Get ye in, lad. Here's mair trouble, maybe.
*(Sebastian goes out by the door on the left. Smollett listens at the main door.* Anither gang o' rowdy wassailers. Duart's makin' a show o' his clansmen to keep the Spaniards in awe, I'm thinking. But they're quarrelsome deils amang themsel's. You're clear noo, Ewan, on the instructions to gi'e to Dol'?

**EWAN**

Yes, yes! You will be flashing the lamp three times.

**SMOLLETT**

*(Going to window with the lamp and demonstrating.)* When the last gabbart comes in wi' the hagbutmen for Loch Sunart, I'll wave it three times across the window, like this. *(Then in consternation.)* Mercy on us! Wha lit the lamp? *(He blows out the light.)*

**EWAN**

I was in the store with it searching for a baling-dish.

**SMOLLETT**

*(Relieved, as he looks from the window.)* There's ower muckle daylight yet for onybody to ha'e noticed. In an 'oor it'll be quite dark. It's cloudy too, an' the mune's hidden. When you were oot wi' the bolls o' meal the day did the Spaniards keep guid watch and ward, think ye?

**EWAN**

Slack, slack, yon ones! Singing and drinking and dancing, and playing wi' the Devil's picture-books! Slack, slack!

#### SMOLLETT

Angus Dubh will be ready wi' his boat in case Dol' has to jump for't?

#### EWAN

Yes, he'll have the skiff handy. Will the English Ambassador, Mr Smollett, have sent the good money now? Dol' was asking?

#### SMOLLETT

Dinna stain the tartan wi' your greed, Ewan. Mind! it's a service you're doing to your clan and country.

#### EWAN

Yes, yes. And I should not be leaving that money to soil your own hands, Mr Smollett.

#### SMOLLETT

*(Tossing a purse on the table.)* There you are, then! The ither hauf when the ship's at the bottom o' the Bay.

*(A knock at the main door.)*

Quick! put that purse oot o' sicht! *(Opening the door.)* It's you, Jonacky. You're late.

*(JONATHAN SMOLLETT comes in. He is a homely-featured, fresh-complexioned young fellow of twenty-two, his confidence and military bearing a little exaggerated. He has been schooled in Edinburgh and has a touch of its manners, his speech being less broad than his father's.*

#### JONATHAN

Well, it's a far cry to Dumbarton town. What hills, what bogs, what moorland torrents!

#### SMOLLETT

To say naething o' the change-hooses by the way, eh? The packman saw ye on the Ridge an hour syne.

#### JONATHAN

*(Laughing.)* News travels fast here. I met Barabel on the Aros Road and stopped for a word wi' her. Good e'en to ye, Ewan.

#### SMOLLETT

I micht ha'e kent there was a lass in't. Ha'e ye letters?

#### JONATHAN

Letters and letters. *(Turning out a pocket.)* And a dispatch frae Holyrood.

#### EWAN

I'll be stepping, Mr Smollett. I'll be back again in a short while.

*(HE goes out by the main door.*

**SMOLLETT**

(*Reading the dispatch*) Um! the *San Juan Bautista*. So, so, Mr Ashby, ye're getting impatient, are ye? But it's nae joke smeekin' oot a wasp's byke.

**JONATHAN**

What's that, father?

**SMOLLETT**

Naething, naething. Ye left a' weel at hame?

**JONATHAN**

Yes, yes. But you mentioned the *San Juan*. What's to be done wi' her?

**SMOLLETT**

Dinna meddle wi' affairs o' State.

**JONATHAN**

But, father, you tell me nothing. It's hard to carry news ower half Scotland, and hear nane. Have ony mair o' the Armada ships come near?

**SMOLLETT**

Never a hull mair, and be thankit! Them an' their crews lie fathoms deep amang the conger-eels and partans that'll pick their skulls as white's the chucky stanes. The Loard's wrath was on them; and it's fearfu' to think what befell them on a coast like this. Hoo the *San Juan* won in here in the mirk is a fair marvel. Howsomever, I dae some guid business victualling her, and shouldna be complaining.

**JONATHAN**

She's a wonderful sight with her high poop and brazen cannon. I'd like to see over her.

**SMOLLETT**

(*Starting*) Ye're no' to steer a foot near her.

**JONATHAN**

Why?

**SMOLLETT**

(*Evasively*) She's a nest o' sedition and treachery. Your life wouldna be safe.

**JONATHAN**

Have you some designs on her? I've heard you say you'd like to see her blown up.

**SMOLLETT**

Aye! But thinkin's ae thing, and daein's anither.

**JONATHAN**

*(Impatiently)* You treat me as if I was a bairn!

**SMOLLETT**

This muckle I may tell ye. Don Sebastian's been bidin' here. His faither—the Commander—sickened a week syne—fever and ague. The young Don brocht him ashore, and I gi'ed them the spare chaumer there. Sebastian was feared that if his faither dee'd the crew would mutiny. Weel, dee he did; and it but to be kept secret. Don Sebastian sits there, in watch by an empty bed, pretending his faither's still deidly ill.

**JONATHAN**

A sad enough task.

**SMOLLETT**

And day and nicht the crew send ashore speiring for the auld ane's health.

**JONATHAN**

Hoping for the worst?

**SMOLLETT**

Gasping for't. And, if Sebastian doesna get the upper haun o' thae desperadoes afore the truth comes oot, it'll be hell let loose on ship and shore. So, you see, I've guid reason in forbidding you to gang on board.

**JONATHAN**

*(Impatiently.)* Others have been shown over the ship, and why not me?

**SMOLLETT**

Noo dinna anger me. I've tell't ye the danger. And there are ither things I'm no' free to speak o'. I'm gaun doon to the quayheid. You'd better come wi' me. You'll get a guid enough sicht o' her there. This wey.
*(As they make for the door on the right,* **SMOLLETT** *has the ship's lantern with him. There comes a knocking at the main door, and* **SMOLLETT** *turns back to peep out of the window, then drops the bar on the main door, and rejoins* **JONATHAN.**

**SMOLLETT**

Juist a beggar-lass. Let us be going.
*(***THEY** *go out by the door on the right. The knocking at the main door continues. After a little* **DON SEBASTIAN** *opens the door on the left, comes down the steps, crosses to the main door and opens it.* **BARABEL MACLEAN** *enters.* **SHE** *is a fair-complexioned, pleasant, handsome girl of eighteen—self-possessed, with a slightly coy air and occasional little bursts of gaiety.* **SHE** *leaves the door unbarred.*

**SEBASTIAN**

Ah, señorita! I was wondering if you would ever return.

**BARABEL**

*(Archly)* Then you were expecting me? Has Jonathan Smollett not arrived yet?

**SEBASTIAN**

Ah! That is the reason you are here?

**BARABEL**

*(Laughing shyly.)* Indeed, then, and you're mistaken! See what I've brought! *(Holding up her basket.)*

**SEBASTIAN**

Flowers! as from a Castilian garden. Things of beauty in this dark, stern land! *Mil gracias, señorita!*

**BARABEL**

*(Smiling.)* Oh! we're not all savages hereabouts. And I've some dainties for your father as well. How is the poor man?

**SEBASTIAN**

*(His hand over his eyes.) Ah, señorita!*

**BARABEL**

Is he worse?

**SEBASTIAN**

No, no, better. Ah, little one! so kind! I cannot lie to you. He is gone.

**BARABEL**

Dead?

**SEBASTIAN**

*Si, señorita.* Since three days. And I am alone now: I feel as if alone in all the world.

**BARABEL**

It's sorry I am to hear this. But you have friends on the ship.

**SEBASTIAN**

The crew is mutinous, and I dare not let them know what has happened, lest they break into open revolt. You, too, must keep it secret.

**BARABEL**

I will surely. Did your father suffer much?

**SEBASTIAN**

In spirit, yes. For always would he cry out in his delirium at our flight
from the English. And he had ever the great storm in mind—the rocks
of the Isles, and the shouts of drowning men—the seas sown with
sunken reefs—wild, beaconless, uncharted seas! Always he cried,
"What shore is that? What shore is that? " It was terrible, truly.

**BARABEL**

The poor man!

**SEBASTIAN**

And he cursed those winds of hell that drove us from the battle he
sought—winds of ten thousand devils that snapped our masts like
reeds. It was that memory brought desolation to his soul. *(Pulling
himself together.)* But I must think of it no longer. I am a soldier, and
have a soldier's tasks before me. Treachery among our own people is
hard to bear.

**BARABEL**

Dare you not go near the ship now?

**SEBASTIAN**

I go on board this evening. The musketeers are friendly. It is they who
are to help your kinsman.

**BARABEL**

It's dying I am to see over that wonderful ship. You spoke of taking me
out.

**SEBASTIAN**

I shall be charmed to escort you.

**BARABEL**

*(Diffidently)* I will have one other favour to ask.

**SEBASTIAN**

But ask a hundred. You have been so kind to my father in his sickness
and solitude.

**BARABEL**

It's to let Jonathan Smollett go with us. He's fell keen to go on board the
galleon.

**SEBASTIAN**

Let him come also, then: the protecting knight errant! He is your
friend—friend of the heart, is it not?

**BARABEL**

*(Shyly.)* He is just the good friend.

**SEBASTIAN**

Ah! But I do not rank so in your thoughts?

**BARABEL**

You are a stranger among us, Don Sebastian. You would surely not be wishing that.

**SEBASTIAN**

*(With gallantry.) Sangre mia!* why not? I come upon a sweet northern flower. Must it only turn to me its thorns?

**BARABEL**

You ken you're only jesting. Have I not heard the tales of the Spanish grandees, and seen the airs of your young officers? What would I be doing among such folk? — a plain country lass?

**SEBASTIAN**

But you are related to the Chief.

**BARABEL**

*(Laughing.)* Oh, we're a' cousins in the Highlands.

**SEBASTIAN**

But it is Nature who is mother of us all and makes us weeds or flowers. To my friends it would be a privilege to meet you.

**BARABEL**

I'm sorry you'll be speaking this way. I canna go with you this evening.

**SEBASTIAN**

Now you desolate me! How can I see you — hear your voice — and remain unmoved? But I have done. There will be no more of this — no more, I swear to you, if you will promise to come. But, if you refuse, then I threaten you, I shall make love to you every hour.

**BARABEL**

*(Brightening up again and laughing.)* I will come, then. But my friend must be coming too.

**SEBASTIAN**

It is agreed. I also will ask a favour. That you include me among your friends.

**BARABEL**

It's a bargain, then, atween us.

**SEBASTIAN**

On my faith I swear it. And to seal it, I kiss your hand.
(*As he does so,* **JONATHAN SMOLLETT** *comes in by the main door.*) Ah, Master Jonathan! You have returned after your long ride. The roads are mountainous and wild? No?

**JONATHAN**

*(Feeling himself eclipsed by the Spaniard's grand airs, and in jealousy resenting this.)* Well, they're no' sae smooth as a ship's quarter-deck.

**SEBASTIAN**

Ah! the quarter-deck has its caprices too. But I see you are tired after your journey, and may have no wish to talk. Yet Mistress Barabel has made up for it. She knows how to comfort the exile, alone and friendless in a strange land.

**JONATHAN**

Nae doot.

**SEBASTIAN**

I go to get my sword and cloak. I will return presently.

*(He goes out by the door on the left.*

**BARABEL**

You're very quiet, Jonathan. What's the matter?

**JONATHAN**

Naething.

**BARABEL**

Oh, then, if you'll be keeping it to yourself —

**JONATHAN**

You seem gey and free wi' the young Don.

**BARABEL**

Oh, it's that! What way should I no'?

**JONATHAN**

It's not what I expected, Barabel.

**BARABEL**

Dinna be foolish, Jonacky. Surely you've something else to talk about after your jaunt to Edinburgh. And, keep me! are you not the gay cavalier in your braw new riding-suit! What a stack o' arms you carry!

**JONATHAN.**

And need for them, too, comin' over the String o' Lorn.

**BARABEL**

I ken. There are roving bands o' broken men, very desperate, on the roads, I'm hearing. I'm glad you won here safe.

**JONATHAN**

So you say.

**BARABEL**

Shame to you now, Jonacky! It's only right we should be kind to Don Sebastian in his loneliness. He's made himself most agreeable.

**JONATHAN**

Agreeable enough. Aye, and I suppose his courtly airs put a plain callant like myself in the shade.

**BARABEL**

And what now have I done that you should be speaking to me this way?

**JONATHAN**

Did I not see him kiss your hand?

**BARABEL**

Jonathan!

**JONATHAN**

I might think lighter o't if I cared for you less.

**BARABEL**

It is not like you to talk this way. If you're going to be so cross over a little thing, we'll have to go out to the ship without you.

**JONATHAN**

(*Amazed.*) Out to the ship!

**BARABEL**

Oh, I havena told you! You put it clean out my head. He's going to show us over the galleon this evening.

**JONATHAN**

You'll surely not go near it?

**BARABEL**

Why will I no'?

**JONATHAN**

At this hour? Among such men? They threaten mutiny. And other things are whispered. You dinna ken the danger, Barabel! I canna allow you to do this.

**BARABEL**

(*Smiling amusedly*) I'll no' be asking your leave. Don Sebastian thinks it a convenient time. There's a full moon rising. The ship will be half empty. You were very anxious to go yourself.

**JONATHAN**

But I've learned what the risks are. I canna see you exposed to them.

**BARABEL**

*(With finality.)* I'm going.

**JONATHAN**

But, Barabel —

> *(DON SEBASTIAN comes in by the door on the left.*

**SEBASTIAN**

The boats are now coming in with the musketeers. We can go out with the last of them as it returns.

**JONATHAN**

*(Still protesting.)* But, Barabel —

**BARABEL**

Yes, I'm ready to go.

> *(Distant pipes are heard playing a coronach.*

**JONATHAN**

Mercy on us! what's that?

**SEBASTIAN**

Ah, the pipes! What slow, sad music!

**BARABEL**

It's a dirge, a lament. It's only played when some chieftain's buried.

**SEBASTIAN**

Then it's for my father! But what rashness, what folly! When I've tried so hard to conceal his death!

> *(JOHN SMOLLETT comes in hastily by the door on the right.*

**SMOLLETT**

What's this I'm hearing? Whatna madness is this?

**JONATHAN**

*(After looking from the main door.)* It's Duart's pipers.

**SMOLLETT**

It maun be his doin'! The big Hielan' stot! I tell't him the Commander's death wud ha'e to be concealed. He hummed and hawed and blew himsel oot, and said his clansmen could keep law and order.

**SEBASTIAN**

It's an act of madness!

**SMOLLETT**

What could we dae again' the guns o' the ship? Sorrow on us that it ever cam' near the port! If the men mutiny, we'll ha'e the hale place tumblin' aboot our ears. We maun ha'e this stoppit instanter.

**JONATHAN**

The seamen are foreigners! They'll maybe no' understand the music.

**SMOLLETT**

Is that a' the college at Embro' has teached ye? Music's a language kent by every tribe and nation.

**SEBASTIAN**

If you can make the pipers change to a gay tune it will allay suspicion.

**SMOLLETT**

Barabel, lass, you ha'e influence wi' Duart. Run up and ask him to gar the pipers play "The Tailor o' Moy" or "Castle Aros". He can swagger and ruffle it just as weel on the like o' them. Haste ye, lass. I'll see Seumas, the heid piper, masel'.

(**BARABEL** and **SMOLLETT** go out.

**JONATHAN**

(Grudgingly.) I'm sorry for this blunder. You've had troubles enough already.

**SEBASTIAN**

I still hope the seamen will prove reasonable. Their nerves were all unstrung by the tempests the ship came through. But it should be quiet on board to-night, once the musketeers are got off.

**JONATHAN**

(Sulkily.) Then you're still bent on going?

**SEBASTIAN**

(Blandly.) Si, señor, I must keep faith with the lady.

**JONATHAN**

Don Sebastian, I don't approve of her going. It's not the time for't. It's not the place to take a young lass. And I've other reasons.

**SEBASTIAN**

What reasons?

**JONATHAN**

You don't need me to tell you the danger. The crew are not to be trusted. Anything may happen. She shouldna be encouraged to go.

**SEBASTIAN**

It has a spice of adventure—nothing more. And it should be left to the señorita to decide.

**JONATHAN**

I think different.

**SEBASTIAN**

If there was any real danger I would warn her before we went on board.

**JONATHAN**

You mayna ken.

**SEBASTIAN**

And do you, my friend?

**JONATHAN**

I've only heard the general rumours, and they're alarming enough. I'd ha'e scruples in going masel'.

**SEBASTIAN**

But why? Unless you are hiding something? *(With a touch of suspicion)*

**JONATHAN**

I ken no more than I've tell't ye. To you—a stranger—it may matter little what happens to her. But it matters a great deal to me.
And I'll not see her jeopardized through any foreigner's whim.

**SEBASTIAN**

How do you know it matters nothing to me?

**JONATHAN**

*(Starting.)* Oh, it does?

**SEBASTIAN**

I have some regard for the lady. *(With a laugh)* But do not make hasty inferences. You are not a chivalrous people. You will not understand. Well, I am a son of Spain, where the service to beauty is a devotion. I meet the *señorita*, who has the loveliness of a wayside flower. I ask no more than the privilege of paying court to her. That is a thing of beauty—an end in itself. I think of nothing beyond.

**JONATHAN**

*(Dourly.)* I ken these flourishes can be made the cloak for rascally acts. No girl I respect will be exposed to the chance o' them.

**SEBASTIAN**

The decision rests with the lady, not with you.

**JONATHAN**

It'll ha'e to be decided between us here and now.

**SEBASTIAN**

But how can you force it?

**JONATHAN**

You'll stop trying to inveigle her on board that ship, or you'll not leave this place alive.

**SEBASTIAN**

*(Suddenly alert.)* You say?

**JONATHAN**

*(Drawing his sword.)* Here's what'll decide for us, if you'll listen to nothing else.

**SEBASTIAN**

Master Jonathan, this is folly. Your surmises are quite wrong. No harm is intended. And sword-play is an art with us. I do not want such an advantage over you.

**JONATHAN**

Is it coward you are as well as rascal? Defend yourself! (**SEBASTIAN** *draws.)* Hide your sword! Here's Barabel!
　　(**THEY** *whip their swords behind them.* **BARABEL** *comes in by the main door.*

**BARABEL**

*(Laughing.)* Is not Duart the great baby! I had to flatter him into changing the tune. I told him the hagbutmen would be fearing to come ashore if he made such a show of strength with his pipers and claymores.

**SEBASTIAN**

You are a born diplomat. We owe you a debt as peacemaker. Is it not so, *caballero?*

**JONATHAN**

It's only prudence to parade the clan. Your musketeers might be tempted to do some mischief if they saw nothing to check them.

**SEBASTIAN**

*(Shrugging his shoulders.)* Master Jonathan is still suspicious. He forgets that it is as friends and allies the musketeers are being disembarked.

**JONATHAN**

It's not the first time that foreign help has proved a danger to those that sought it.

**BARABEL**

The soldiers arena landing at all. They are going aboard Duart's birlinns, and many are already half across to Sunart.

**SEBASTIAN**

Master Jonathan is not to be satisfied. Also, he disapproves of your going out to the ship.

**BARABEL**

*(Disappointed.)* Oh! And will you not be for taking me?

**JONATHAN**

I told him I'm opposed to it—at this hour—and among such men.

**SEBASTIAN**

It is for the lady to choose!

**JONATHAN**

I think not. We've already argued that.

**SEBASTIAN**

I bow to the *señorita*'s will.

**JONATHAN**

*(Darkly.)* You'll not listen to me, then?

**SEBASTIAN**

*(Smiling.)* But I am not at your command.

**BARABEL**

*(Laughing.)* Fine, fine! I'll have you crossing swords for me, like knights in the tourney.

**SEBASTIAN**

We could not devote them to a worthier office.

**BARABEL**

You'll be making me the envy o' every lass on the Isle. But what for do you both stand so stockish wi' your hands behind you? There's little o' the knightly in that, I'm thinking.
  (**SEBASTIAN** *succeeds in leaning his sword against a table behind him, and*
  *comes forward, folding his arms.*

**SEBASTIAN**

It is for you to decide. We submit ourselves to your will.

**JONATHAN**

*(Desperately.)* Barabel, I entreat you!

**BARABEL**

I'm for going, then. You make too much o' the danger, Jonathan. I want to see this great ship. It'll no' take long. Indeed we'll have to be stepping. It's late enough already.

**JONATHAN**

*(Grimly.)* Then I'll go too.
  (*He tries to lean his sword behind him as* **SEBASTIAN** *has done, but it tilts*
  *along the table, striking the other, and both crash to the floor.*

**BARABEL**

*(Starting, and in consternation.)* Oh! you had your swords drawn!

**SEBASTIAN**

*(Calmly, as he lifts his own.)* Si, señorita. We were comparing them, as soldiers do. And, curiously enough, they are both Toledo make.

**BARABEL**

*(In wonder and some alarm.)* Only that?

**JONATHAN**

Yes, we were trying their temper when you appeared.

**SEBASTIAN**

But, as you say, we must hasten. It is late.

**BARABEL**

*(Hesitating.)* Well —

**JONATHAN**

We needna delay longer.
> *(As* **BARABEL** *goes out by main door she looks back with apprehension.* **JONATHAN** *and* **SEBASTIAN** *sheathe their swords, and offer each other precedence in going after her.*

**SEBASTIAN**

*(With a courtly bow.)* Señor!

**JONATHAN**

*(Bowing stiffly.)* Sir!
> *(Finally* **SEBASTIAN** *goes out,* **JONATHAN** *following.* **JOHN SMOLLETT** *comes in by the door on the right. Jonathan halts at sight of him.*

**SMOLLETT**

Weel, Jonacky, you're oot and in a lot—just as restless as a whittruck, eh? Weel, oot ye gang noo, and stay oot; for I've private business the nicht *in*side.

**JONATHAN**

Have ye that, indeed? ... Weel, I've private business the nicht, but it's *oot*side.
> *(***HE** *goes off angrily, banging the door.*

**SMOLLETT**

Come in, Ewan. The place is clear. Bring the lamp wi' ye.
> *(***EWAN,** *with lit lamp, comes in by the door on the right.*
I'll wave it masel'. Bring it here, man. What ails ye? *(***HE** *takes the lamp from him.)*

#### EWAN

I'll no' be wanting you to show that light.

#### SMOLLETT

(Startled.) What's this?

#### EWAN

It's Torquil, the Chief's foster-son. They have put him also on board the ship.

#### SMOLLETT

I ken. Anither hostage for the safe return o' the hagbutmen.

#### EWAN

A good lad, and a MacKinnon. Of my own clan, look you!

#### SMOLLETT

He'll ha'e to take his chance along wi' Dol' MacLean, then! They'll devise some plan o' escape, I'll warrant.

#### EWAN

You can wait for another evening, Mr Smollett. I will not be liking this at all, at all.

#### SMOLLETT

We'll ne'er get sic anither chance, aince the Loch Sunart men come back. The thing maun be dune, and dune withoot delay. Besides, ye've been weel paid for't.

#### EWAN

Paid for, is it? (He loses his temper and gabbles angrily at Smollett in Gaelic.) Mhic a'choin! Sasunnach, suarach, salach! Mallachd ort!

#### SMOLLETT

Stop you, stop! Nane o' that gibberish! I dinna understaun' a word o't.

#### EWAN

There's your dirty money. I'll not be touching a farthing o't. (He throws down the purse.)

#### SMOLLETT

Oh, you Hielandmen, you Hielandmen! Ye hing by ilk ither like wolves on the trail! Weel, you can clear oot o' this!

#### EWAN

I will be asking you not to make that signal this night.

**SMOLLETT**

Ask awa'! It's noo or never! Every 'oor that ship lies there is a threat to our lives. And besides, they're the Kirk's and God's enemies; and can be weel dune withoot. *(Going to the window.)* They're running up a riding-licht on the foremast. But here's ane that'll send them on their langest cruise.

**EWAN**

Och! sorrow on you!

**SMOLLETT**

If Torquil wasna on the ship, he'd be oot on the foray, and no' a whit safer there. He maun just tak' his chance. Ye canna spare the buck for the fleas on't. And ye've a saying in the Isle here, " Lat the tail gang wi' the hide". Weel, lat it gang!

*(HE makes to pass the lamp across the window. EWAN seizes it and blows it out. SMOLLETT, enraged, strikes him with his staff. EWAN makes to draw his oxter knife; but SMOLLETT catches his dirk hand with his own left, and with his right takes him by the throat.*

Whit! Ye'd draw your dirk on me? Drap it, or I'll thraw your neck!

*(EWAN drops the knife, and SMOLLETT throws him against some sacks of meal. HE then takes up the lamp and examines it.*

Ye've spilt the lamp ile; and I'll ha'e to replenish. Noo, dinna interfere again, my mannie, if ye value your life.

*(SMOLLETT goes out by door on the right. EWAN lurches to the window and looks out. DON SEBASTIAN enters by the main door.*

**SEBASTIAN**

Pardon me! I take one of the candles. But why are you so pale? Are you ill?

**EWAN**

No, just a wee turn, and the roomity pains.

**SEBASTIAN**

I am sorry. I will bring this back in a moment.

*(HE goes out by the door on the left, and presently returns with the candle and some papers.*

**EWAN**

I wonder now, will you be going out to the ship?

**SEBASTIAN**

Yes. I should have gone earlier, but there is some trouble. The sailing-master disputes my authority. I take to him my father's written orders. Master Jonathan has gone out on the pinnace with him.

**EWAN**

Jonathan!

**SEBASTIAN**

Yes. Why are you so alarmed? He only went out because of the trouble among my men— to see if it were safe for Mistress Barabel to go aboard the galleon.

**EWAN**

And Barabel is still ashore then?

**SEBASTIAN**

Yes. Mistress Barabel is still ashore. You fear for Master Jonathan?

**EWAN**

His father'll no' be liking it.

**SEBASTIAN**

No. Mr Smollett is very suspicious. You can tell him his son is perfectly safe.

**EWAN**

Yes, yet. Perfectly safe—perfectly safe

**SEBASTIAN**

I may not return till late.
(**HE** *goes out by the main door, and* **SMOLLETT** *re-enters on the right, with the lamp re-lit.*

**SMOLLETT**

(*Cautiously.*) Was that Don Sebastian I heard?

**EWAN**

Yes. He's gone off to the ship.

**SMOLLETT**

Ah! He'll never mair set fute on her. I had to trim the lamp again— wasting precious time! Noo, Ewan, keep you oot o' this, or it'll be the waur for ye! I'm acting under orders frae Holyrood, and it'll be a serious thing if you intermeddle again.

**EWAN**

Oh, I'll not be meddling with you any more, Mr Smollett. For, look you! I'll not be forgetting you have the strong arm for striking. Oh, yes, Mr Smollett, I'll be standing aside.

**SMOLLETT**

You're showing some sense at last, then. Dol' MacLean, whilst firing that magazine—like the brave man he is—is taking his life in his haun's. Torquil's in nae waur case. Be sure they'll try some pliskie to win clear.

**EWAN**

Yes, yes. Torquil will have to take his chance, whatever!
> *("Four Bells" is heard to strike on board the ship.*

**SMOLLETT**

Listen! Fower bells! Six o'clock! Their last watch! *(Glancing from the window.)* Eh, sirs, it's little they think it's their ain death-knell they're ringing. Weel, weel, it's the fires o' the Inquisition they'd ha'e brocht on us. And sae the deep waters, o' the Bay can tak' them. *(He waves the lamp thrice across the window.)*
*(Excitedly.)* Dol' has seen't! He's showing a licht at the port-hole amidships! And noo may the Loard ha'e mercy on their souls!

**EWAN**

Aye! And on your own soul, my pretty man! *(He is smiling sardonically.)*

**SMOLLETT**

*(Puzzled by his enigmatic smile.)* On mine?

**EWAN**

Yes! And on Torquil MacKinnon and Jonathan Smollett.

**SMOLLETT**

What? What's that?

**EWAN**

*(Triumphantly.)* I'm saying Jonathan! He went out wi' the young officers to see over the galleon. Don Sebastian was telling me.

**SMOLLETT**

*(Distractedly.)* Jonathan! Ha'e mercy, Loard! *(He rushes to the window.)* What can I do to put a stop on them!
> *(A dull roar is heard reverberating over the hills and waters. The window-panes are shattered.* **SMOLLETT** *sinks groaning to the table, his face covered with his hands, his fingers in his ears.*

Too late! Jonathan! Jonathan!
> *(The door is suddenly dashed open and* **BARABEL** *rushes in, and, falling on her knees beside the old man, hides her face in his lap, and sobs piteously.*

**CURTAIN**

# Man of Uz

DEDICATED TO
JAMES BRIDIE

**REFERENCES:**
TEXTS AND COMMENTARIES

*The Book of JOB* (Authorized Version): A. B. DAVIDSON: University Press, Cambridge.
*Lectures on JOB* (Revised Version): G. G. BRADLEY: Clarendon Press, Oxford.
*The Book of JOB* (Revised Version): S. R. DRIVER: Clarendon Press, Oxford.
*The Original Poem of JOB* (Translated from the Restored Text): E. J. DILLON: Fisher Unwin, London.
*The Book of JOB* (Short Studies on Great Subjects: Vol. I): J. A. FROUDE: Longmans, London.
*The Modern Reader's Bible*: R. G. MOULTON: Macmillan, London.
*The Bible, Designed to be Read as Literature:* ERNEST SUTHERLAND BATES: Heinemann, London.

**THE BOOK OF JOB**
Magnificent and sublime as no other book of Scripture.— LUTHER.

There is nothing written, I think, in the Bible or out of it, of equal literary merit.—CARLYLE.

The greatest poem whether of ancient or modern times.—TENNYSON.

What, in all the thousands of sermons, and theologies, and philosophies with which Europe has been deluged, has been gained for mankind beyond what we have found in this book of JOB?—FROUDE.

PERSONS

NAHOR
ELIPHAZ
BILDAD
ZOPHAR
JOB

About 500 B.C.: A Day in Spring:

# The Syrian Desert

*SCENE.—The confines of the Syrian Desert in the darkness of a simoon. The sound of the storm gradually dies away, and the light increases slowly until a blue sky of unbroken serenity is seen stretching to the bare rose-coloured hills on the horizon. From these the desert sands extend to some rocks in the foreground. On the left are some ruins, with a single palm tree. Close to these is a tent, alike in details to the Bedouin tent of to-day. It is made of woven goat-hair; the front curtains are drawn up, and it can be seen that some compartments in the interior are walled off by hanging cloths. A water-pot stands in a corner beside several bowls of brass and a camel saddle. On the floor are some rugs and blankets made of material coloured in stripes of black, green, maroon and white. The tent is set at an angle, facing forwards.*

*On the right the rocks ascend to form a cliff with a narrow gully.*

*Towards the centre is a mound, and on it are spread rugs and blankets similar to those in the tent.*

*There is a sound of* **VOICES** *on the right, and* **NAHOR**, *a prophet, followed by* **ELIPHAZ, BILDAD** *and* **ZOPHAR**, *come down the gully, and approach the tent cautiously.*

**NAHOR** *is a man of forty, alert, athletic, and clad in the simple white tunic of the peasant. His bearing, however, suggests something more than the peasant: it is that of a man who feels the power within, which, when the hour comes, makes him prophet.* **ELIPHAZ** *appears to the first glance as carrying all the benignant airs of a wise old age.* **BILDAD** *looks the practical man, the traditionalist.* **ZOPHAR***'s main traits are those of a man unsure of himself and determined, therefore, to assert his certainty about everything.*

*(As* **THEY** *enter.*

### ELIPHAZ
Nay, let the Prophet speak. He hath known JOB of old.

### NAHOR
... And it fell on a day that there came a messenger unto JOB, and said: "Your sons and your daughters were eating and drinking wine in their eldest brother's house; and, behold, there came a great wind from the wilderness, and smote the four corners of the house, and it fell upon the young men, and they are dead; and I only am escaped alone to tell you."

*(All bow their heads; and after a silence* **NAHOR** *continues:*

### NAHOR
Then JOB arose, and rent his mantle, and shaved his head, and fell down upon the ground, and worshipped, and he said: "Naked came I out of my mother's womb, and naked shall I return thither: the Lord gave, and the Lord hath taken away; blessed be the name of the Lord." In all this JOB sinned not, nor charged God foolishly.

**ELIPHAZ**

Blessed be the name of the Lord!

**NAHOR**

But again there came a day, and JOB was smitten with sore boils from the sole of his foot unto his crown. And he took a potsherd to scrape himself withal; and he sat among the ashes. Then said his wife unto him: "Do you still hold fast your integrity? Renounce God, and die." But he said unto her: "You speak as the foolish women speak. Shall we receive good at the hand of God, and shall we not receive evil?" ... In all this JOB did not sin with his lips.

**ELIPHAZ**

Blessed be the name of the Lord!

(JOB *appears from behind one of the hangings in the tent.* HE *recognises his friends, makes a gesture of despair, and staggering to the mound with its heap of camel-rugs, subsides on it.* HE *is emaciated, his face pale; his clothing a rough gown that leaves arms and legs bare. His friends seat themselves around him, and bow their heads in silence.* NAHOR *withdraws towards the ruined wall; at times he turns his eyes heavenwards, and at times scans the faces of the men before him as if seeking in their eyes the vision himself would see.*

**BILDAD**

Let us mourn with him.

**ZOPHAR**

Let us comfort him.

(*They sprinkle dust upon their heads.*

**JOB**

Let the day perish wherein I was born;
And the night which said: "There is a man child conceived!"
Let that day be darkness;
Let not God regard it from above,
Neither let the light shine upon it!
Let darkness and the shadow of death claim it for
their own;
Let a cloud dwell upon it;
Let all that maketh black the day terrify it!

**ELIPHAZ**

(*Interrupting.*) If we essay to commune with you, will you be grieved? But who can withhold himself from speaking?

**JOB**

(*Unheeding.*) Lo, let that night be barren;
Let no joyful voice come therein!
Let the stars of the twilight thereof be dark!

Let it look for light, but have none;
Neither let it behold the eyelids of the morning;
Because it shut not up the doors of my mother's womb,
Nor hid trouble from mine eyes.

ELIPHAZ

Behold, you have instructed many,
And you have strengthened the weak hands.
Your words have upheld him that was falling,
And you have confirmed the feeble knees.
But now this has come upon you, and you faint;
It touches you, and you are troubled.
Is not the fear of God your confidence,
And your hope the integrity of your ways?
Remember, I pray you, who ever perished, being
innocent?
Or where were the righteous cut off?
According as I have seen, they that plow iniquity,
And sow trouble, reap the same.
By the breath of God they perish,
And by the blast of his anger are they consumed.

JOB

Why died I not from the womb?
Why did the knees receive me?
Or why the breasts, that I should suck?
For now I should have lien down and been quiet;
I should have slept; then had I been at rest,
With kings and counsellors of the earth,
Who built solitary towers for themselves;
Or as an hidden untimely birth I had not been;
As infants which never saw the light.
There the wicked cease from troubling;
There the weary be at rest.
There the prisoners are at ease together;
They hear not the voice of the taskmaster.

ELIPHAZ

Now a thing was secretly brought to me,
And mine ear received a whisper thereof.
In thoughts from the visions of the night,
When deep sleep falleth upon men,
Fear came upon me and trembling,
Which made all my bones to shake.
Then a spirit passed before my face;

The hair of my flesh stood up.
It stood still, but I could not discern the form thereof;
There was silence, and I heard a voice saying:
"Shall mortal man be more just than God?
Shall a man be more pure than his Maker?
Behold, he putteth no trust in his servants;
And his angels he chargeth with folly:
How much more them that dwell in houses of clay,
Whose foundations are in the dust!
Betwixt morning and evening they are destroyed:
They perish for ever without any regarding it.
Their tent-cord is plucked away from them;
They die, and that without wisdom."

**JOB**

Wherefore is light given to him that is in misery
And life unto the bitter in soul?
Which long for death but it cometh not;
And dig for it more than for hid treasures;
Which rejoice exceedingly,
And are glad when they can find the grave.

**ELIPHAZ**

As for me I would seek unto God,
And unto God would I commit my cause:
Behold, happy is the man whom God correcteth:
Therefore despise not the chastening of the Almighty.
For he maketh sore, and bindeth up;
He woundeth, and his hands make whole.
He shall deliver you in six troubles;
Yea, in seven there shall no evil touch you.
In famine he shall redeem you from death;
And in war from the power of the sword.
You shall come to the grave in a full age,
Like as a shock of corn cometh in in its season.
Lo this, we have searched it, so it is;
Hear it, and know it for your good.

**JOB**

Oh that my grief were but weighed,
And my calamity set in the balance against it!
For now it would be heavier than the sand of the seas.
Therefore my words are wild.
For the arrows of the Almighty are within me,
And my spirit drinks up their venom:
The terrors of God do set themselves in array against me.

Oh that I might have my request;
And that God would give me the thing I long for,
Even that it would please God to crush me;
That he would let loose his hand and cut me off!
Then should I yet have comfort;
Yea, I would exult in pain that spareth not:
For I have not denied the words of the Holy One.

### BILDAD

*(In anger.)* How long will you speak these things?
How long shall the words of your mouth be like a
mighty wind?
Doth God pervert Judgment?
Doth the Almighty corrupt justice?
If you would seek diligently unto God,
And make supplication to the Almighty;
If you were pure and upright, surely now he would awake for you,
And make the house of your righteousness prosperous.

### JOB

What is my strength, that I should wait?
What is mine end, that I should be patient?
Is my strength the strength of stones?
Or is my flesh of brass?
I have no help in me;
Sound wisdom is driven quite from me.
To him that is afflicted pity should be shewed by his friend;
Even to him that forsaketh the fear of the Almighty.
My brethren have dealt deceitfully as a brook,
As the channels of brooks that pass away;
Which are black by reason of the ice,
And wherein the snow hideth itself:
What time they wax warm, they vanish:
When it is hot, they are consumed out of their place.
The caravans that travel by the way of them turn aside;
They go up into the waste and perish.
The caravans of Tema looked,
The companies of Sheba waited for them.
They were ashamed because they had hoped;
They came thither, and were confounded ...
As for you, ye are nothing;
Ye see a terror, and are afraid ...
Teach me, and I will hold my peace;
And cause me to understand wherein I have erred.

How forcible is all your talk about uprightness!
But what does your arguing reprove?
What use to rebuke words?—
Words of the desperate, spoken to the wind!
You, who would cast lots upon the fatherless,
And make merchandise of your friend! ...
Now therefore be pleased to look upon me ...
Am I a liar? ...
Return, I pray you, and let no wrong be done me;
Yea, return again; my cause is righteous ...
Is there not a warfare to man upon earth?
And are not his days like the days of a hireling?

### BILDAD

Inquire, I pray you, of the former age,
And apply yourself to that which their fathers searched out;
Shall they not teach thee, and tell thee,
And utter words out of their heart ...
Can the rush grow up without mire?
Can the reed grow without water?
Whilst yet in its greenness, and not cut down,
It withereth before any other herb.
So are the paths of all that forget God;
And the hope of the godless man shall perish.

### JOB

(*Unheeding* BILDAD.)
When I lie down, I say: "When shall I arise?"
But the night is long;
And I am full of tossings to and fro
Unto the dawning of the day.
My flesh is clothed with worms and clods of dust;
My skin closeth up and breaketh out afresh.
My days are swifter than a weaver's shuttle,
And are spent without hope.

(ALL *bow their heads before the fire of his words.*
JOB *raises his hands in supplication to heaven, and speaks again.*

### JOB

Am I a sea, or a monster of the sea,
That thou settest a watch over me?
When I say: "My bed shall comfort me,
My couch shall ease my complaint";
Then thou scarest me with dreams,
And terrifiest me with visions:

So that my soul chooseth strangling,
And death rather than these my bones.
I loathe my life; I would not live alway;
Let me alone;
For my days are vanity ...
What is man, that thou shouldest magnify him,
And that thou shouldest set thine heart upon him,
And that thou shouldest visit him every morning,
And try him every moment?
How long wilt thou not look away from me,
Nor let me alone till I swallow down my spittle?
If I have sinned, what can I do unto thee, O thou watcher of men?
Why hast thou set me as a mark for thee,
So that I am become a burden to myself?

*(The OTHERS make signs of protest at this outburst.*

### BILDAD

*(Repeating his last words mechanically.)*
"The hope of the godless man shall perish."
*(Then eagerly.)*
He is green before the sun, and his shoots go forth over his garden;
But his roots are wrapped about a heap of stones, and the rock keeps hold on him.
It destroyeth him from his place,
And denying him saith: "I have not seen thee."
Lo, God will not cast out a blameless man,
Neither will he take evil-doers by the hand.

### JOB

Of a truth I know that it is so;
But how can a man be in the right with God?
If he desire to contend with God,
He cannot answer one of his thousand riddles.
God is wise in heart, and mighty in strength:
Who hath hardened himself against him, and prospered ...
Against him who removeth the mountains, and they know it not,
When he overturneth them in his anger?
He shaketh the earth out of her place,
And the pillars thereof tremble.
He commandeth the sun and it riseth not;
And sealeth up the stars.
He alone stretcheth out the heavens,
And treadeth on the waves of the sea.
He maketh Arcturus, Orion, and the Pleiades,

And the chambers of the south.
He doeth great things past finding out;
Yea, marvellous things without number ...
Lo, he goeth by me, and I see him not:
He passeth on, but I perceive him not.
Behold, he taketh away, and who can hinder him?
Who will say unto him: "What doest thou?"
If I supplicate, it is to a judge,
Who doth not answer, though I am righteous;
Who would sweep me away with a tempest,
And multiply my wounds without cause.
He will not suffer me to take my breath,
But filleth me with bitterness.

### ZOPHAR
Should not this multitude of words be answered?
And should a man full of talk be justified?
Should your lies make men hold their peace?
And when you mock shall none make you ashamed?

### JOB
*(Continuing as if he had not heard* ZOPHAR.*)*
If we speak of strength, lo, he is strong!
And if of judgment, who shall challenge him?
Though I were just, my own mouth would condemn me:
Though I were faultless, he would make me crooked.
I put my life at stake, and will speak out;
It is all one now ...
Therefore I say: He destroyeth the upright as well as the wicked,
And his scourge slayeth blindly.
He mocketh at the sorrows of the innocent.
The earth is given unto the hand of the wicked,
He covereth the faces of the judges thereof ...
If it be not HE,
WHO then is it?

### ZOPHAR
O, that God would speak,
And open his lips against you ...
Know therefore that God exacteth of you
Less than your iniquity deserveth!

### JOB
*(Unheeding* ZOPHAR.*)*
Now my days are swifter than a post:
They flee away, they see no good.

They are passed away as the swift ships:
As the eagle that swoopeth on the prey ...
(*Looking upwards.*)
If I wash myself with snow water,
And make my hands never so clean:
Yet thou wilt plunge me in the ditch,
And mine own clothes shall abhor me ...
(*Turning to* ZOPHAR.)
Would he were a man, that I might answer him,
That we might come together in judgment!
Would there were an umpire between us,
Who would lay his hand upon us both! ...
Let him take his rod away from me,
And let not dread of him make me afraid,
Then would I speak and not fear him;
For in myself is no cause for fear ...

### ZOPHAR

Do you say unto God: "My doctrine is pure,
And I am clean in thine eyes"?

### JOB

My soul is weary of my life;
I will give free course to my complaint;
I will speak in the bitterness of my soul.
I will say unto God: Do not condemn me.
Shew me wherefore thou contendest with me.
Is it meet that thou shouldest oppress?
(*He looks upward.*)
That thou shouldest thrust aside the work of thine hands,
And shine upon the counsel of the wicked?
Seest thou as man seeth?
Are thy days as the days of mortals?
For thou inquirest after mine iniquity,
And searchest after my sin,
Although thou knowest I am not wicked,
And there is none that can deliver out of thine hand.
Thine hands have framed me
And fashioned me together round about;
Yet thou dost destroy me!
Remember, I pray thee, that thou hast fashioned me as clay;
And wilt thou bring me into dust again?
Hast thou not clothed me with skin, and flesh,
And knit me together with bones and sinews?

Thou hast granted me life and favour,
And thy care hath preserved my spirit.
And yet these things thou didst hide in thine heart! ...
I know that this was in thee!
If I be wicked, woe unto me!
Yet if I be righteous, I dare not lift my head ...
As a fierce lion thou huntest me,
And ever thou shewest thyself marvellous upon me!
Thou smitest me anew,
And thy wrath waxeth great against me ...
Wherefore then didst thou bring me forth from the womb?
Are not my days few?
Cease then, and let me alone,
That I may take comfort a little,
Before I go whence I shall not return:
Even to the land of darkness and of the shadow of death:
A land of thick darkness, as darkness itself;
A land of the shadow of death, without any order;
And where the light is as darkness.

### ZOPHAR

Can you by searching find out God?
Can you find out the Almighty unto perfection?
His wisdom is high as heaven;
What can you do?
Deeper than Sheol;
What can you know?
The measure thereof is longer than the earth,
And broader than the sea.
If he pass through, and shut up,
And call to judgment, then who can hinder him?
For he knoweth vain men;
He seeth iniquity where man considers there is none.
But vain man is void of understanding:
Yea, void as the wild ass's colt ...
But if you set your heart aright,
And stretch out your hands towards him,
Then shall you lift up your face,
You shall be steadfast, and shall not fear:
You shall forget your misery;
And remember it as waters that are passed away.
Though there be darkness, it shall be as the morning;
And your life shall be clearer than the noonday.
You shall lie down, and none shall make you afraid.

No doubt but ye are the people,
And wisdom shall die with you! ...
But I have understanding as well as you;
I am not inferior to you:
Yea, who knoweth not such things as these? ...
I am just and upright, not a wild ass's colt!
And you who are at ease laugh at misfortune:
Your contempt is ready for one whose foot slippeth.
Yes, you laugh, though the tents of the robbers prosper,
And they that provoke God are secure ...
But ask now the beasts, and they shall teach you;
And the fowls of the air, and they shall tell you;
Or, speak to the earth, and it shall teach you;
And the fishes of the sea shall declare unto you:
Is not the soul of every living thing in God's hand,
And the breath of all mankind?
Behold, he breaketh down,
And it cannot be built again;
He shutteth up a man,
And there can be no opening.
Lo, he withholdeth the waters,
And they dry up.
Again he sendeth them out,
And they overwhelm the earth.
With him is strength and wisdom;
The deceived and the deceiver are his.
He leadeth counsellors away barefoot,
And judges maketh he fools.
He looseth the bond of kings;
And overthroweth the nobles.
He withdraweth the speech of the trusty,
And taketh away the understanding of the aged.
He poureth scorn upon princes,
And looseth the girdle of the strong.
He discovereth deep things out of darkness,
And bringeth the shadow of death unto light.
He taketh away the heart of the chiefs of the earth,
And maketh them to wander in a pathless wilderness.
They grope in the dark without light,
And stagger to and fro like drunken men ...
Lo, mine eye hath seen all this,
Mine ear hath heard and understood it.

What ye know, the same do I know also.
Again I say, I am nowise inferior unto you.

Are you the first man that was born?
Or were you brought forth before the hills?
Were you heard in the secret council of God?
And have you drawn wisdom unto yourself?
What know you that we know not?
What understanding have you that is not in us?

Surely I would speak to the Almighty,
And I desire to reason with God ...
But ye are forgers of lies,
Ye are all physicians of no value.
Oh, that ye would altogether hold your peace!
And it should be your wisdom ...
Hear now my reasoning,
And hearken to the pleadings of my lips ...
Will ye speak unrighteously for God,
And utter lies on his behalf?
Will ye accept his person by trickery?
Will ye contend for God with falsehood?
Well for you if he searched you out!
Can ye deceive him as ye deceive men?
Shall not his majesty make you afraid,
And his dread fall upon you?
Your fine sayings are proverbs of ashes,
And your arguments defences of clay ...
Hold your peace, let me alone, that I may speak,
And let come on me what will!
At all adventures I will take my flesh in my teeth,
And put my life in mine hand.
Though he slay me, yet will I wait for him:
Nevertheless I will maintain my ways before him.
And this shall be my salvation,
That a godless man shall not appear in his sight.

Are the consolations of God too small for you,
And the word that dealeth gently with you?
Why doth your heart carry you away?
And what do your eyes wink at?
Why do you turn your spirit against God,

And let such words go out of your mouth? ...
Behold, he putteth no trust in his holy ones;
Yea, the heavens are not clean in his sight.
How much less one foul and corrupt,
A man that lappeth up iniquity like water!
                (**NAHOR**, *in the background, clenches his hands, as if in despair at the
                                                        obtuseness of* **ELIPHAZ**.

**JOB**

Behold now I have ordered my cause;
And I know that I shall be justified...
*(He raises his hands to heaven.)*
Withdraw thine hand from me,
And let not dread of thee make me afraid!
Then call thou and I will answer,
Or let me speak and answer thou me ...
How many are mine iniquities?
Make me to know my transgressions.
Wherefore hidest thou thy face,
And holdest me for thine enemy?
Wilt thou harass a leaf driven to and fro?
And wilt thou pursue the dry stubble?
For thou writest down bitter things against me,
And imputest to me the errors of my youth.
Thou markest all my paths,
And fastenest my feet in the stocks ...
Man that is born of woman
Is of few days, and full of trouble;
He cometh forth like a flower, and is cut down,
He fleeth also as a shadow and continueth not.
And dost thou open thine eyes upon such an one!
And bringest him into judgment with thee!
Though he is like a rotten thing that consumeth,
Like a garment that is moth-eaten!
For there is hope of a tree, if it be cut down, that it will sprout again,
And that the tender branch thereof will not cease ...
But man dieth and wasteth away:
Yea, man giveth up the ghost, and where is he?
As the waters fail from the sea,
And the river decayeth and drieth up,
So man lieth down and riseth not;
Till the heavens be no more he shall not awake ...
Oh, that thou wouldest hide me in Sheol,
That thou wouldest keep me in secret until thy wrath be past!
That thou wouldest appoint me a set time, and remember me!

... If a man die, shall he live again? ...
All the days of my warfare I then would wait, till my release should come;
Thou shouldest call, and I would answer thee;
Thou wouldest have a desire to the work of thine hands! ...
But now thou numberest my steps:
Dost thou not watch over my sin?

### ELIPHAZ

The wicked man travaileth with pain all his days,
Even the number of years that are laid up for the oppressor.
A sound of terror is in his ears;
In prosperity the spoiler shall come upon him.
Distress and anguish make him afraid;
They prevail against him, as a king ready to the battle;
Because he hath stretched out his hand against God,
And behaveth himself proudly against the Almighty,
And rusheth upon him with a stiff neck,
Under the thick bosses of his buckler ...
But let him not trust in vanity, deceiving himself:
For vanity shall be his recompense.
His offshoot shall wither before his time,
And his branch shall not be green.
He shall shake off his unripe grape like the vine,
And shall cast his flower like the olive.
For the company of the godless shall be barren,
And fire shall consume the tents of bribery.

### JOB

(Sighing.) I have heard many such things:
Miserable comforters are ye all! ...
I also could speak as you do,
If your soul were in my soul's stead;
I could heap up words against you,
And shake mine head at you.
I too could give you comfort—
Comfort like yours: from the lips outward ...
But God hath wearied me that I am benumbed;
His whole host hath seized me;
He hath torn me in his wrath, and pursued me;
He hath gnashed upon me with his teeth.
I was at ease, and he brake me asunder;
Yea, he hath taken me by the neck, and dashed me to pieces:
He sets me up for his mark;
His archers compass me round about.

He breaketh me with breach upon breach;
He runneth upon me like a giant ...
I have sewed sackcloth upon my skin,
And have laid my horn in the dust.
My face is foul with weeping,
And on my eyelids is the shadow of death;
Although there is no violence in mine hands,
And my prayer is pure ...
O earth, cover thou not my blood!
And let my cry have no resting place!
Even now, behold, my witness is in heaven,
And he that voucheth for me is on high ...
My friends scorn me;
But mine eye poureth out tears unto God ...
As for you all do you try again: come now!
And I shall not find one wise man among you.
My days are past, my purposes are broken off,
Even the thoughts of my heart.
If I still have hope, it is for Sheol.
I have spread my couch in the darkness;
I have said to corruption: "Thou art my father!"
And to the worm: "Thou art my mother and sister!" ...
Where then is my hope?
My hope ...?... Who shall see it?
It shall go down to the bars of Sheol,
Where there is rest in the dust.

### BILDAD

How long ere you make an end of words?
Consider, and afterwards let us speak ...
Wherefore are we counted as beasts,
Reputed vile in your sight?
Shall the earth be deserted because of you?
And shall the rock be removed from its place?
Nay; but the light of the wicked shall be put out,
And the spark of his fire shall not shine.
The light shall be dark in his tent,
And the lamp above him put out.
Terrors shall make him afraid on every side,
And shall chase at his heels.
His strength shall be hungerbitten,
And calamity shall be ready for his halting ...
His remembrance shall perish from the earth;
And he shall have no name in the street.

He shall be driven from light into darkness,
And chased out of the world.
He shall have neither son nor son's son among his people,
Nor any remaining where he sojourned.
They that come after shall be astonished at his day,
As they that went before were affrighted.
Such, surely, are the dwellings of the unrighteous,
And this is the place of him that knoweth not God.

JOB

How long will ye vex my soul,
And break me in pieces with words!
Know now that God hath subverted me in my cause,
And hath compassed me with his net.
Behold I cry aloud, but I am not heard;
I cry for help, but there is no judgment.
He hath fenced up my way that I cannot pass;
He hath stripped me of my glory.
Mine hope hath he felled like a tree:
His troops throng together, and block my way.
He hath put my brethren far from me;
Mine own familiar friends are estranged from me.
They that dwell in my house, and my maids, count me for a stranger;
I am an alien in their sight.
I call my servant, and he giveth me no answer,
Though I intreat him with my mouth.
My breath is strange to my wife,
And they whom I loved are turned against me.
My bones cleave to my flesh,
And I am escaped by the skin of my teeth.

ZOPHAR

Know you not this of old time,
Since man was placed upon earth,
That the triumphing of the wicked is short,
And the joy of the godless but for a moment?
Though his excellency mount up to the heavens,
And his head reach unto the clouds,
He shall fly away as a dream, and shall not be found:
The eye which saw him shall see him no more.
For he hath oppressed and forsaken the poor;
He hath violently taken away a house which he builded not.
There was nothing left that he devoured not,
Therefore his prosperity shall not endure.

*(It is clear from the gestures of* **NAHOR**, *that he is greatly incensed by the words of* **ZOPHAR**; *but he is silent.*

**JOB**

Have pity, have pity upon me, O my friends!
For the hand of God hath smitten me!
Why do you persecute me like God,
And are not satisfied with the woes of my flesh? ...
O that my words were now written!
O that they were inscribed in a book!
That with an iron pen and lead
They were graven in the rock forever! ...
For I know that my vindicator liveth,
And, at the last, shall stand up for me,
Although it be upon my dust.
*(The ecstasy of the vision has been too great for him, and He faints, muttering:)*
My reins are consumed within me ...!

*(The* **OTHERS** *move towards him, but it is plain from their furtive movements that they are repelled by his disease.* **NAHOR**, *however, overcomes his distaste, and bends over* **JOB**, *raising bis head, and adjusting rugs to support his shoulders.* **JOB** *seems to recover after a little, looks round in dazed fashion, sees* **ZOPHAR**, *and instantly the old fire returns. He struggles to his knees, and pointing a minatory finger at* **ZOPHAR**, *says:*

**JOB**

*(Continuing.)* That ye may know there is a judgment ...

**ZOPHAR**

*(Interrupting.)* God shall cast the fierceness of his wrath upon the
wicked,
And shall rain it upon him while he is eating.
He shall flee from the iron weapon,
And the bow of brass shall strike him through.
A fire not blown by man shall devour him.
The heavens shall reveal his iniquity,
And the earth shall rise up against him ...
This is the portion of a wicked man from God.

**JOB**

Then wherefore do the wicked live,
Become old, yea, wax mighty in power?
Their houses are safe from fear,
Neither is the rod of God upon them.
Their bull gendereth, and faileth not;
Their cow calveth, and casteth not her calf.

They send forth their little ones like a flock,
And their children dance.
They sing to the timbrel and harp.
And rejoice at the sound of the pipe.
They spend their days in prosperity.
And go down gently to the grave.
Yet they say unto God: "Depart from us,
For we desire not the knowledge of thy ways.
What is the Almighty that we should serve him?
And what profit should we have if we pray unto him?"

### ELIPHAZ

(Interrupting.) Lo, their prosperity is not in their hand:
The counsel of the wicked be far from me!

### JOB

How oft is it that the lamp of the wicked is put out?
That their calamity cometh upon them?
That they are as stubble before the wind,
And as chaff that the storm carrieth away?

### BILDAD

God layeth up the wicked's iniquity for the wicked's children.

### JOB

Let him rather requite the wicked himself that he may feel it.
Let the wicked see his own destruction with his own eyes,
And let him drink of the wrath of the Almighty.

### ZOPHAR

Shall any teach God knowledge,
Seeing he judgeth those that are high?

### JOB

(Bitterly.)
And yet the breasts of the wicked are full of milk,
And their bones rich in marrow;
While the guiltless die in bitterness of soul,
And never taste any good:
Wicked and righteous alike, they lie down together in the dust,
And the worm covereth them. ...

(ZOPHAR and BILDAD are about to interrupt; but JOB continues, waving them
aside.

### JOB

Behold I know your thoughts,
And the devices by which you think to mislead me.

In vain you try to comfort me,
Since in your answers there remaineth only falsehood.

**ELIPHAZ**

Is it any pleasure to the Almighty that you are righteous?
Is it gain to him that you make your ways perfect?
Is it for your fear of him that he reproves you,
That he enters with you into judgment?
Is it not rather that your wickedness is great?
Are not your iniquities without end? ...
For you have taken pledges from your brother for nought,
And stripped the naked of their clothing;
You have not given water to the weary to drink,
And have withholden bread from the hungry ...
Ah, JOB was indeed the mighty man, the honourable!
The earth and all its fruits were his!...
Yet he has sent widows empty away,
And the arms of the fatherless have been broken! ...
Therefore snares are round about you,
And sudden fear falls on you ...
See you not the darkness,
And the abundance of waters that covers you? ...
Doth not God look down from the height of heaven,
And crush the strong that are become haughty? Acquaint now yourself
with him and be at peace. Thereby shall good come unto you.
Receive, I pray you, the law from his mouth,
And lay up his words in your heart.

**JOB**

O that I knew where I might find him,
That I might come even unto his seat!
I would order my cause before him,
And fill my mouth with arguments.
I would fain know the words which he would answer me,
And understand what he would say unto me ...
Would he contend with me in the greatness of his power?
Surely not ... Let him but give heed unto me;
Then the upright might reason with him;
So should I be delivered for ever from my judge... Behold I go forward,
but he is not there;
And backward, but I cannot perceive him.
But he knoweth the way that I take;
When he hath tried me, I shall come forth as gold.
My foot hath held fast to his steps;

I have not gone back from the commandment of his lips.
Yet he is bent on one thing, and who can turn him?
Therefore am I troubled before his face;
When I consider, I am afraid of him.
God hath made my heart faint;
And darkness covereth my face.

**ELIPHAZ**

If you return to the Almighty, you shall be restored;
If you put away unrighteousness far from your tents,
Then shall you delight yourself in God,
And lift up your face unto him.
You shall make prayer unto him, and he shall hear you;
And you shall pay your vows.
All your purposes shall prosper,
And a light shall shine upon your ways.

**JOB**

If there are days of judgment set by the Almighty,
Why do not they who know him see his days? ...
The wicked remove the landmarks;
They violently take away flocks, and lead them to pasture.
They drive away the ass of the fatherless,
They take the widow's ox for a pledge.
They turn the needy out of the way:
The poor of the earth cower together in hiding;
The wilderness yieldeth them food for their children.
They glean the vintage of the wicked;
They lie all night naked without clothing.
They are wet with the showers of the mountains,
And embrace the rock for a shelter.
Men groan from out the populous city,
And the soul of the wounded crieth out ...
Yet God regardeth not the wrong ...
If it be not so, who will make me a liar!

**BILDAD**

Dominion and fear are with him;
He maketh peace in his high places.
Is there any number to his armies?
And upon whom doth not his light arise?
How then can a man be just before God?
Or how can he be clean that is born of woman?
Behold even the moon hath no brightness,
And the stars are not pure in his sight:

How much less man, that is a worm!
And the son of man, which is a worm!

JOB

How have you helped him that is without power!
How have you upheld the arm that hath no strength!
To whom are you speaking?
What oracle's voice comes from your mouth? ...
As God liveth, who hath taken away my right,
And the Almighty, who hath vexed my soul,
Never shall my lips confess untruth,
Neither shall my tongue utter deceit.
God forbid that I should justify you;
Till I die I will not give up my integrity;
My righteousness I hold fast, and will not let go;
My heart doth not reproach any one of my days.

ZOPHAR

What is the hope of the godless when God cutteth him off?
When he taketh away his soul?
Will God hear his cry, when trouble cometh upon him?
Will he delight himself in the Almighty;
And call upon God at all times?
If his children be multiplied, it is for the sword;
And his offspring shall not be satisfied with bread.
Those that remain of him shall be buried in death,
And their widows shall make no lamentation.

JOB

O that I were as in the days of old,
As in the days when God watched over me,
When his lamp shined upon my head,
And by his light I walked through darkness;
As I was in the ripeness of my days,
When the secret of God was upon my tent;
When I went forth to the gate unto the city,
When I prepared my seat in the street,
The young men saw me and hid themselves,
And the aged rose up and stood;
The princes refrained from talking,
And laid their hand on their mouth;
The voice of the nobles was hushed,
And their tongue cleaved to the roof of their mouth ...
For when the ear heard me, then it blessed me;
And when the eye saw me, it gave witness unto me:

Because I delivered the poor that cried,
The fatherless also, that had none to help him.
The blessing of him that was ready to perish came upon me:
And I caused the widow's heart to sing for joy ...
I put on righteousness and it clothed me:
My justice was as a robe and a diadem.
I was eyes to the blind, and feet was I to the lame.
I was a father to the needy,
And the cause of him that I knew not I searched out.
And I broke the jaws of the unrighteous,
And plucked the prey out of his teeth ...
Unto me men gave ear and waited,
And kept silence at my counsel.
After my words they spoke not again,
And my speech fell upon them like freshening showers ...
But now the young men have me in derision,
Whose fathers I disdained to set with the dogs of my flock:
Children of fools, yea, children of base men;
They were scourged out of the land ...
And now I am become their song,
Yea, I am become a byword unto them.
They abhor me, they stand aloof from me,
And spare not to spit in my face ...
As through a wide breach they come,
In the midst of ruin they roll themselves upon me.
Terrors are turned upon me,
They chase mine honour as the wind;
And my welfare is passed away as a cloud.

**ZOPHAR**

Though the godless heap up silver as the dust,
And prepare raiment in abundance;
He may prepare it, but the just shall put it on,
And the guiltless shall divide the silver.
The wicked lieth down rich, but rich he shall not remain.
Terrors take hold of him like waters;
And a tempest sweepeth him away in the night.

**JOB**

(*Unheeding.*)
In the night season my bones are pierced in me,
And the pains that gnaw me take no rest.
He hath cast me into the mire,
And I am become like dust and ashes.

*(He raises his eyes to the sky, and lifts his feeble hands.)*
I cry unto thee, and thou dost not answer me;
Thou art turned to be cruel to me:
With the might of thy hand thou persecutest me,
And thou dissolvest me in the storm.
For I know that thou wilt bring me to death.
And to the house appointed for all living ...
But shall not a drowning man stretch out his hand?
Shall he not cry out in his destruction? ...
Did not I weep for him that was in trouble?
Was not my soul grieved for the needy?
But when I looked for good, then evil came;
And when I waited for light, there came darkness ...
I go mourning without the sun;
I stand up in the assembly, and cry for help.
My skin is black and falleth from me,
And my bones are scorched with heat.
Therefore is my harp turned to mourning,
And my pipe into the voice of them that weep.

### ZOPHAR

*(Repetitive.)* Terrors take hold of him like waters;
And a tempest sweepeth him away in the night.

### JOB

If I have walked with vanity,
And my foot hath hasted to deceit,
Let me be weighed in an even balance,
That God may know mine integrity ...
If my step hath turned out of the way,
Then let my seed be rooted out.
If mine heart have been enticed unto a woman,
If I have laid wait at a neighbour's door,
If I did despise the cause of my manservant,
Or of my maidservant, when they contended with me:
What then shall I do when God riseth up?
And when he visiteth, what shall I answer him? ...
Never have I withheld the poor from their desire,
Nor caused the eyes of the widow to fail;
Nor have I eaten my morsel alone,
Unless the fatherless had partaken thereof ...
If I have seen any perish for want of clothing,
Or lifted my hand against the fatherless,
Then let my shoulder fall from the shoulder-blade,

And mine arm be broken from the bone ...
If I have made gold my hope;
If I have been a sun-worshipper, or a moon-worshipper,
I should have lied to God who is above.
If I rejoiced at the destruction of him that hated me;
If I opened not my gates to the stranger;
If, like Adam, I covered my transgressions ...
If ... if ... O that I had one to hear me!
(**HE** *again raises his eyes; and his voice has in it appeal and defiance.*)
Lo, here is my signature; let the Almighty answer me!
O that I had the indictment which mine adversary hath written!
Surely I would carry it on my shoulder;
I would bind it unto me as a crown!
I would declare unto him the number of my steps;
And as a prince would I come into his presence!

(*The* **OTHERS** *bow their heads as if abased. Then* NAHOR *stands forth and faces*
**JOB**. *He speaks like a man in a dream: his vocation of Prophet has claimed him.*

### NAHOR

Behold, the Lord doth answer thee out of the whirlwind! ...
Behold, thus saith the Lord:
(**HE** *pauses as if overwhelmed by his message. His ecstasy increases, and he*
*speaks with assurance of the power within.*)
"Who is this that darkeneth counsel
By words without knowledge?
Gird up now thy loins like a man;
For I will demand of thee, and declare thou unto me.
Where wast thou when I laid the foundations of the earth?
Declare if thou hast understanding.
Who determined the measures thereof, if thou knowest?
Or who stretched the line upon it?
Whereupon were its foundations fastened?
Or who laid the corner stone thereof,
When the morning stars sang together,
And all the sons of God shouted for joy?
Or who shut up the sea with doors,
When it broke forth and issued from the womb;
When I made the cloud the garment thereof,
And thick darkness a swaddling band for it,
And prescribed for it my decree,
And set it bars and portals,
And said: 'Hitherto shalt thou come but no further:
And here shall thy proud waves be stayed'? ...
Hast thou commanded the morning since thy days began?

And caused the dayspring to know its place;
That it might take hold of the ends of the earth,
And the wicked be shaken out of it?
For then the earth changes as clay under the seal,
And all things stand forth as on a garment ...
Hast thou entered into the springs of the sea?
Or walked in the abysses of the deep?
Have the gates of death been revealed unto thee?
Or hast thou seen the doors of the shadow of death? ...
Hast thou comprehended the breadth of the earth?
Declare, if thou knowest it all ...
Doubtless thou knowest, for thou wast then born,
And the number of thy days is great! ...
Where is the way to the dwelling of light?
And, as for darkness, where is its abode?
Hast thou entered the granaries of the snow?
Or hast thou seen the treasuries of the hail,
Which I have reserved against the time of trouble,
Against the day of battle and war?
By what means is the mist parted,
And the east wind scattered upon the earth?
Who hath cleft a channel for the rain-flood,
Or a path for the lightning of thunder?
Out of whose womb came the ice?
And who hath brought forth the hoar-frost of heaven,
When the waters are hidden as with a stone,
And the face of the deep is frozen?
Canst thou bind the cluster of the Pleiades?
Canst thou loose the bands of Orion? ...
Canst thou send lightnings that they may go,
And say unto thee: 'Here we are'?
Canst thou hunt her prey for the lioness?
Or fill the hunger of the young lions,
When they couch in their dens,
And abide in the covert to lie in wait? ...
Who provideth the raven with his food,
When his young ones cry unto God,
And wander for lack of meat? ...
Canst thou mark when the hinds do calve?
Canst thou number the months that they fulfil?
They bow themselves, they bring forth their young;
They cast out their sorrows;
Their young ones are in good liking,

They grow up in the open field,
They go forth and return not again ...
Who hath sent out the wild ass free?
Whose house I have made in the wilderness,
Who scorneth the tumult of the city,
Neither heareth the driver's cry...
Will the wild-ox be content to serve thee?
Or will he abide by the crib?
Wilt thou trust him because his strength is great?
Or wilt thou leave thy labour to him? ...
The wing of the ostrich rejoiceth;
But are her pinions and feathers kindly?
For she leaveth her eggs on the earth,
And forgetteth that the foot may crush them.
She is hardened against her young ones, as though
they were not hers:
Though her labour be in vain, she is without fear;
What time she lifteth up herself on high,
She scorneth the horse and his rider ...
Hast thou given the horse his strength?
Hast thou clothed his neck with thunder?
Hast thou made him to leap as a locust?
The glory of his nostrils is terrible.
He paweth in the valley, and rejoiceth in his strength:
He goeth out to meet the armed men.
He mocketh at fear and is not affrighted;
Neither turneth he back from the sword.
The quiver rattleth against him,
The glittering spear and the javelin.
He swalloweth the ground with fierceness and rage;
Neither standeth he still at the sound of the trumpet.
He saith among the trumpets: 'Ha, ha';
And he smelleth the battle afar off,
The thunder of the captains and the shouting ...
Doth the hawk soar by thy wisdom,
And stretch out her wings to the south? ...
Doth the eagle mount up at thy command,
And make her nest on high?
She dwelleth on the rock, and hath her lodging there,
Upon the crag of the rock and the stronghold.
From thence she spieth out the prey;
Her eyes behold it afar off.
Her young ones also suck up blood:

And where the slain are, there is she ...
(NAHOR *halts for a space, as if listening to the inner voice, then continues:*)
Moreover, the Lord answereth JOB:
Thus saith the Lord:
"Shall he that cavilleth, contend with the Almighty?
He that argueth with God, let him answer.
Gird up thy loins now like a man:
I will demand of thee, and declare thou unto me ...
Wilt thou even disannul my judgment?
Wilt thou condemn me, that thou mayest be justified?
Or hast thou an arm like God?
If thou canst thunder with a voice like his,
Deck thyself now with excellency and grandeur,
And array thyself with honour and majesty.
Pour forth the rage of thy wrath:
Hurl down every one that is proud and abase him ...
Look upon every one that is proud and bring him low;
Trample down the wicked where they stand.
Hide them in the dust together;
Bind their faces in secret ...
Then will I also confess of thee
That thine own right hand can save thee."
(*He bows his head.*)
      (**JOB** *rises and turns his face heavenwards. He is transfigured by the vision of*
*the greatness of the earth and all that it contains. God has made no direct reply*
      *to all his questionings; yet he has been answered in the deeps of his being.*
                  *When he speaks, it is in a spirit of rapt contemplation.*

### JOB
Behold, I am of small account; what shall I answer thee?
I lay mine hand upon my mouth.
Once have I spoken, but I will not answer;
Yea, twice, but I will not again ...
I know that thou cast do all things,
And that no purpose of thine can be restrained ...
Hence, I say, I have uttered that I understood not, Things too
wonderful for me, which I knew not.
(*Speech fails him for a little, and* **HE** *bows his head; then looks up again, a new*
*light in his eyes.*)
I have heard of thee by the hearing of the ear:
But now ... mine eye ... seeth thee!
(*It is sunset now, and the twilight darkens rapidly: but one clear ray strikes up*
                                                                    *the sky.*
   **ELIPHAZ** *gazes at* **JOB** *with startled eyes, as if he comprehended something of*

*his ecstasy.*
**BILDAD**, *hand on lip, is puzzled and uneasy.*
**ZOPHAR** *is quite clearly bored, and stares in bovine fashion at nothing at all.*
**JOB** *stands erect, transfigured, his eyes uplifted.*

## CURTAIN

# Note

This Play should only be performed by trained speakers of verse.

To readers unfamiliar with the stage, the introduction of such a figure as that of NAHOR may appear—to say the least—an unwarrantable intrusion in this—or any— adaptation of so great a masterpiece of art as the Book of JOB. In reality it is here a necessity, since this is a stage-adaptation. And for this reason: no voice off-stage is so clearly heard as that from a speaker visible to the audience (other things, like pitch and volume, being equal).

From long experience this conclusion is axiomatic with playwrights, players, producers, and the keener playgoers.

And experience also indicates that the closer proximity to the audience of the on-stage speaker compared with that of the off-stage speaker is not the prime factor in the matter.

The explanation seems to be that all our senses act in unison, if in varying degrees; but that eye and ear are more closely linked by the central nervous system than any of the other sense-organs.

It is therefore Nature herself that here makes demands on Art. We cannot loose the bands of Orion.

J.B.

www.ingramcontent.com/pod-product-compliance
Lightning Source LLC
Chambersburg PA
CBHW060052100426
42742CB00014B/2791